Celtic Mandala Coloring Book

Celtic Adult Coloring Book containing 40 beautiful Celtic Knot Mandala

by The Coloring Book People

ISBN-13: 978-1523652501

ISBN-10: 1523652500

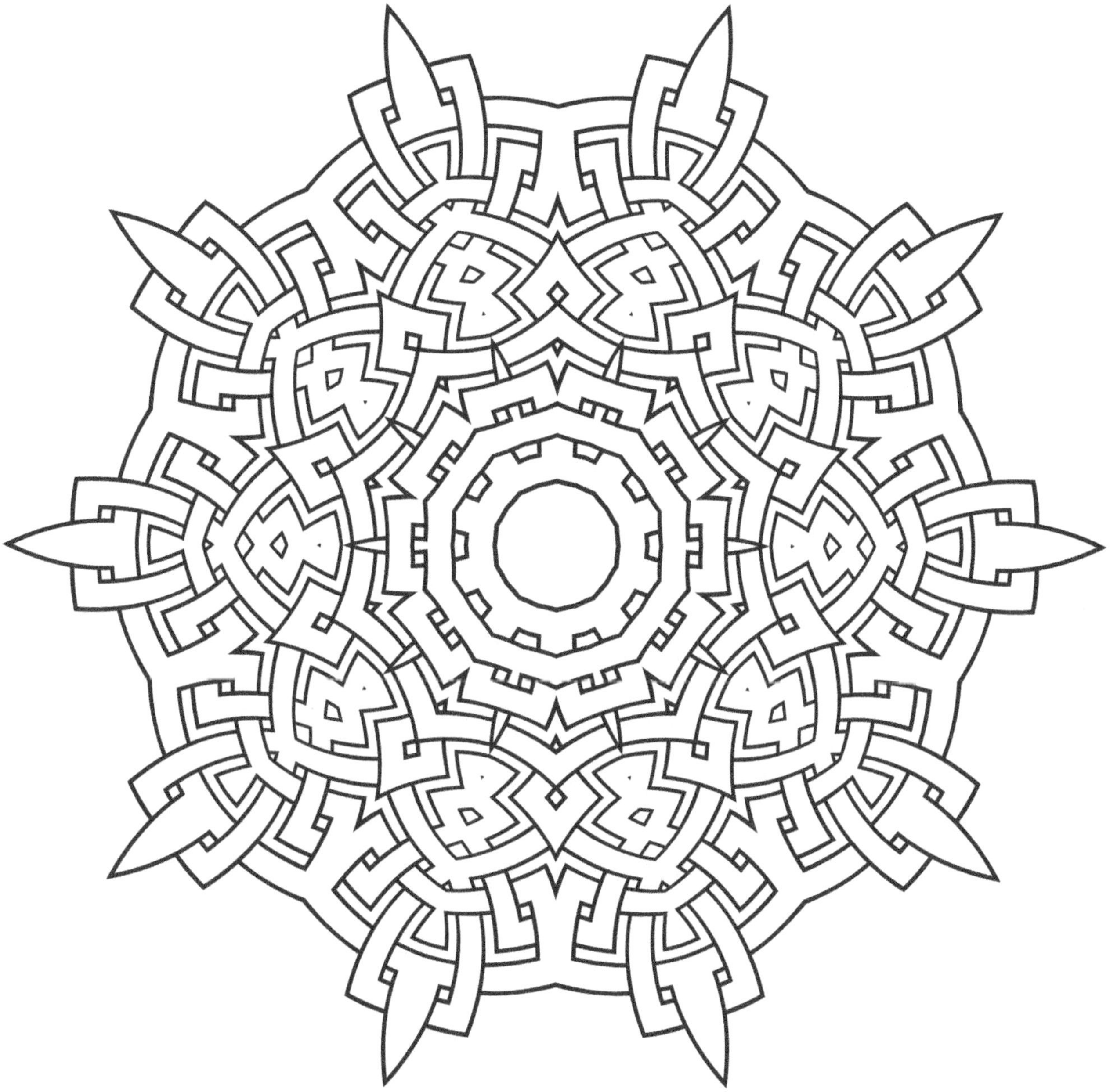

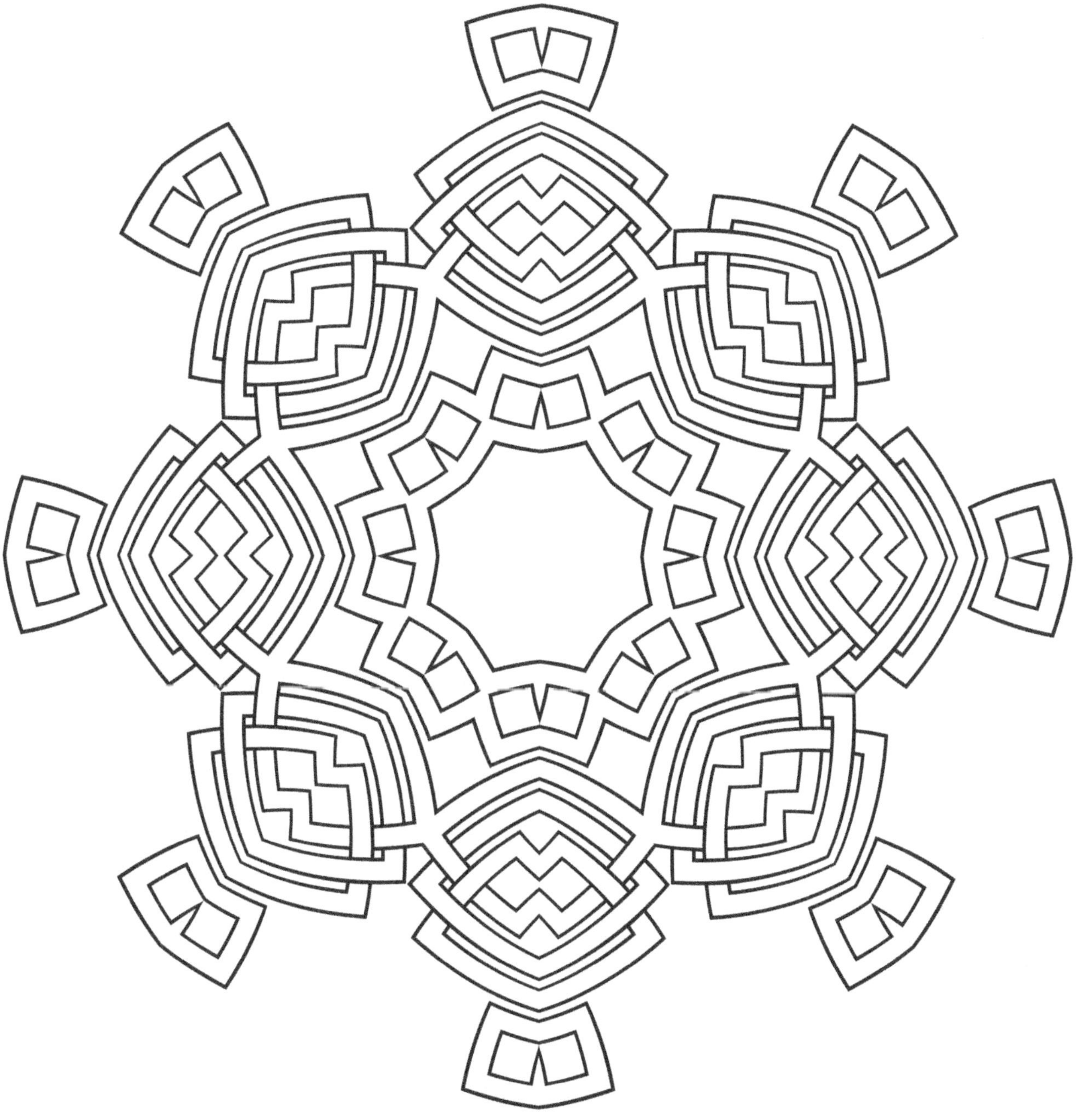

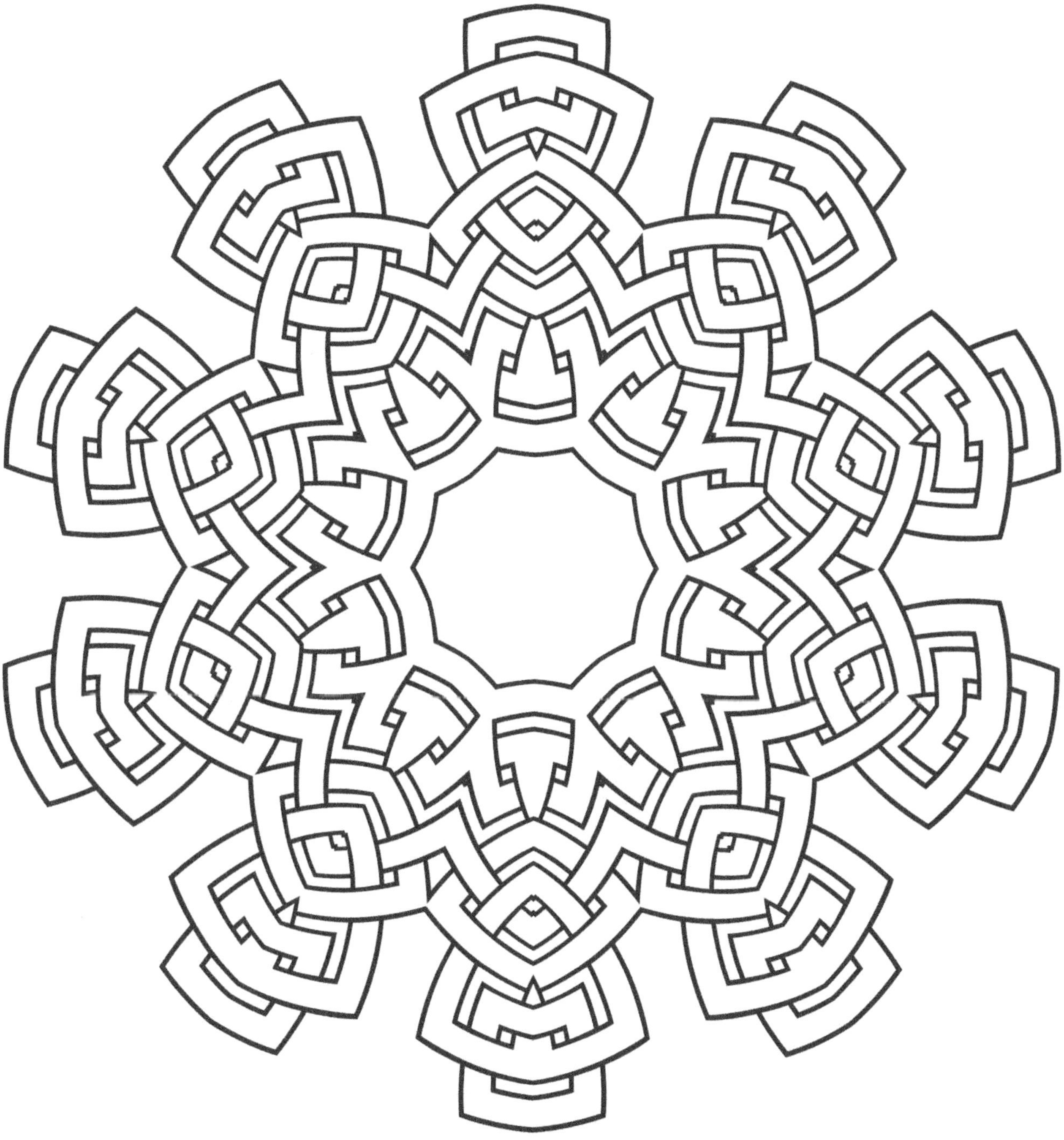

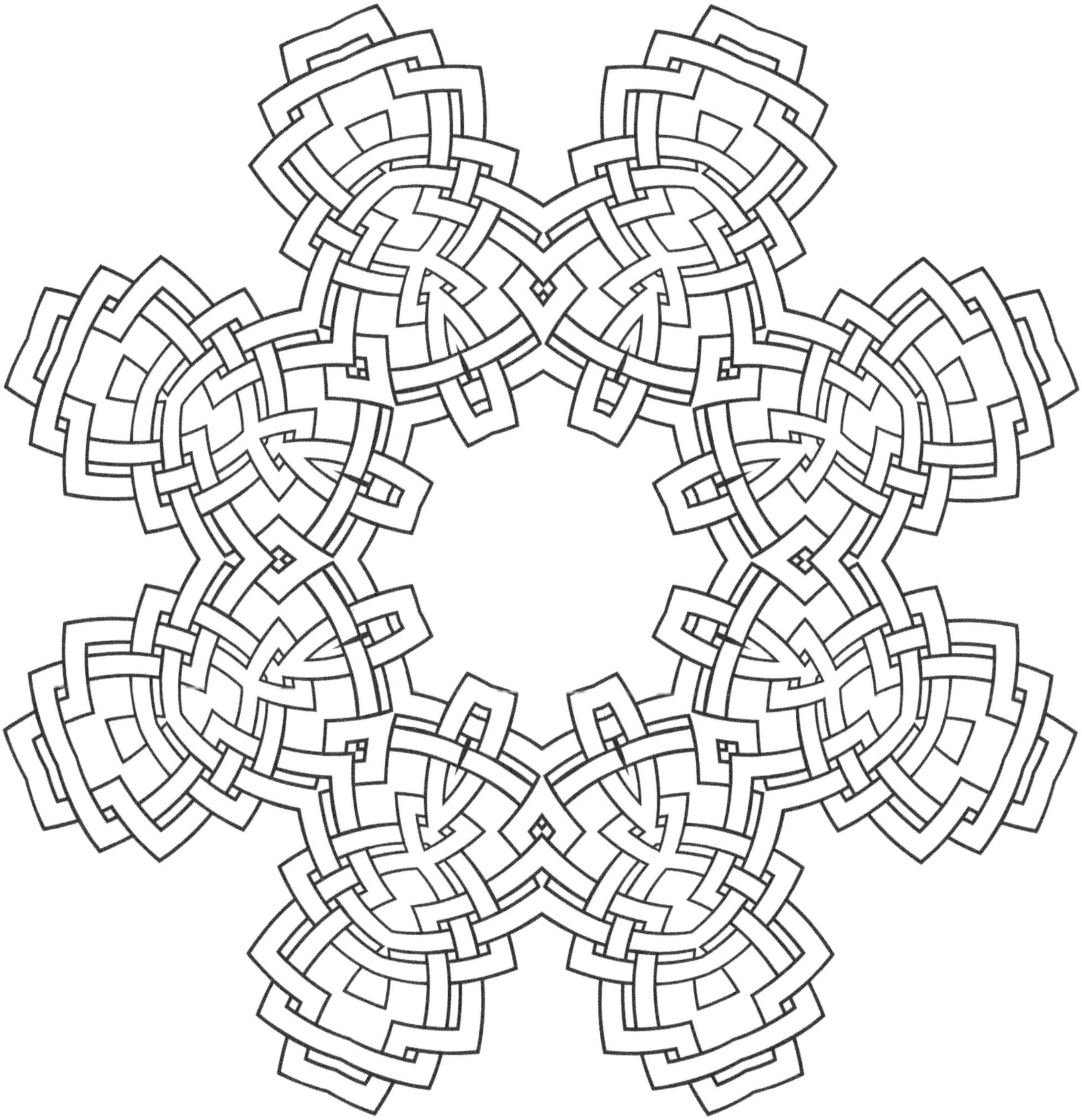

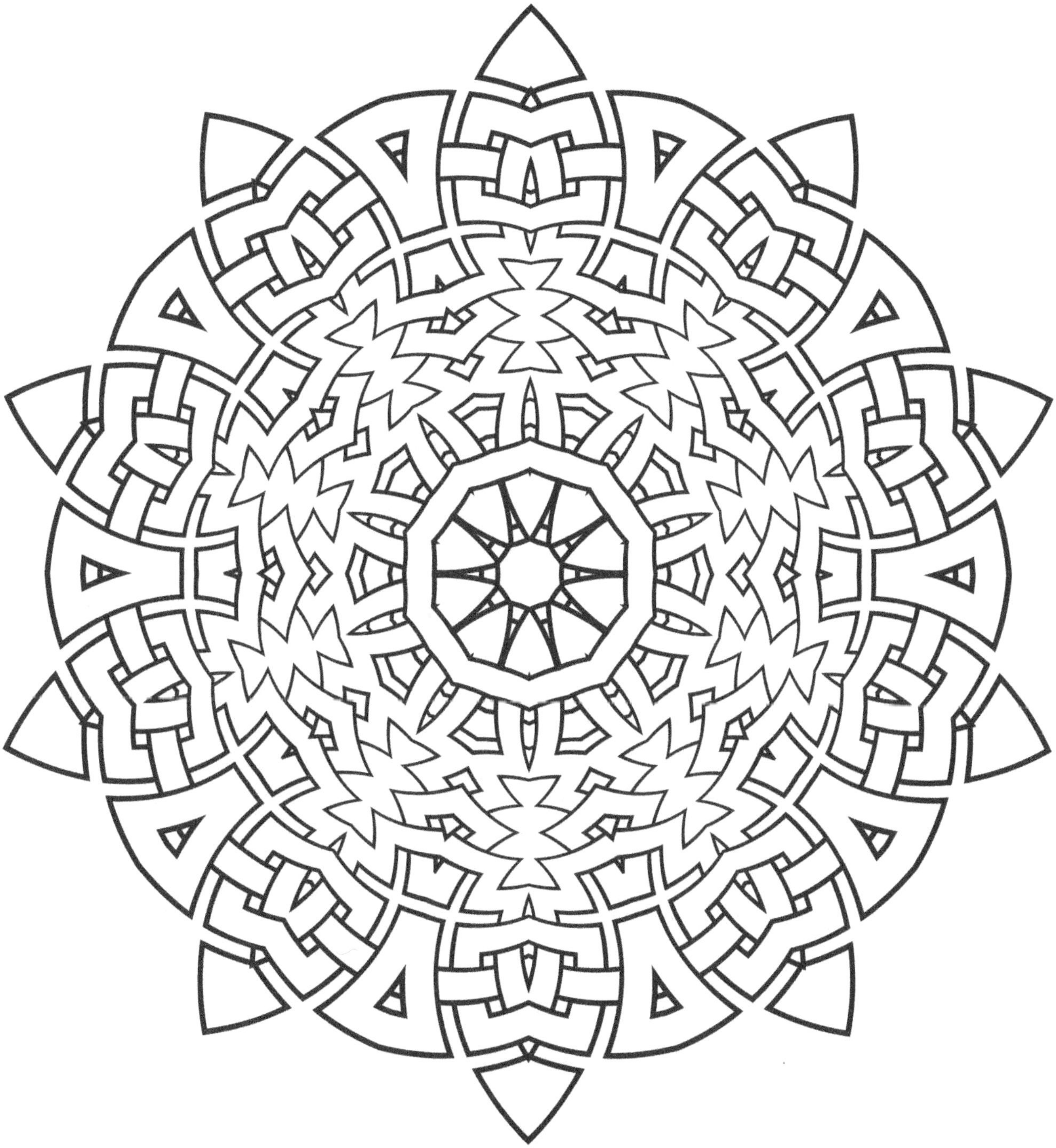

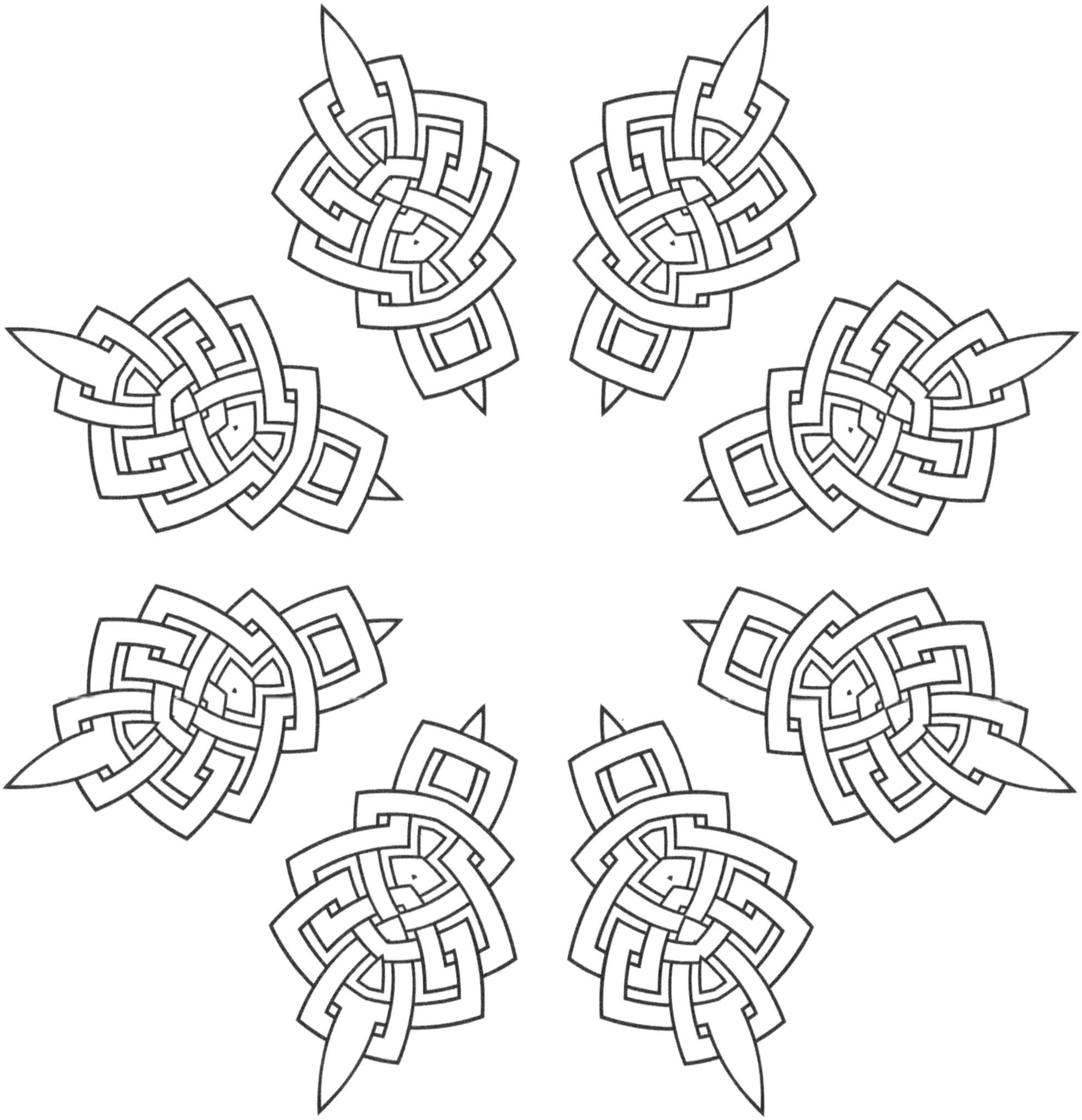

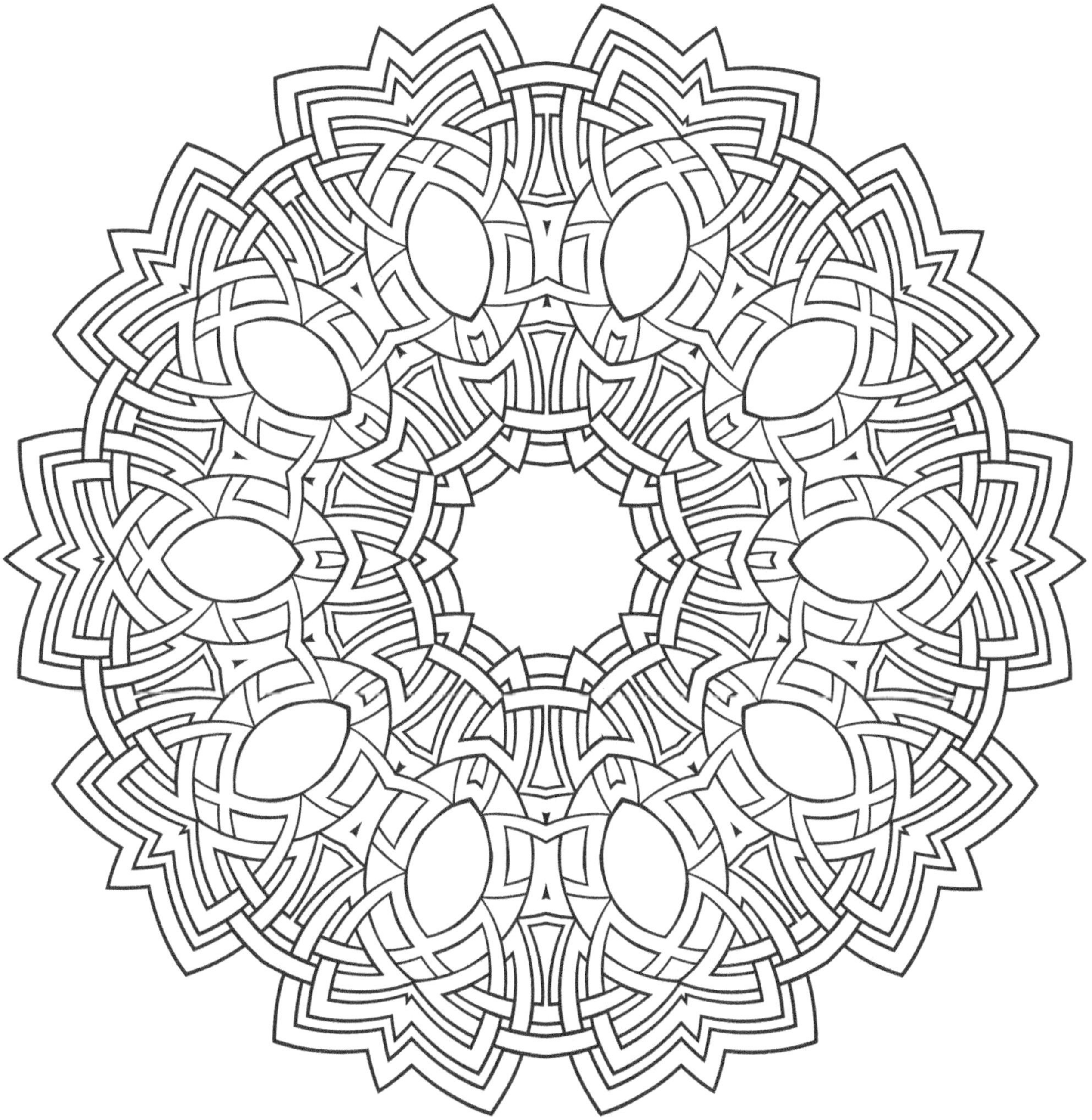

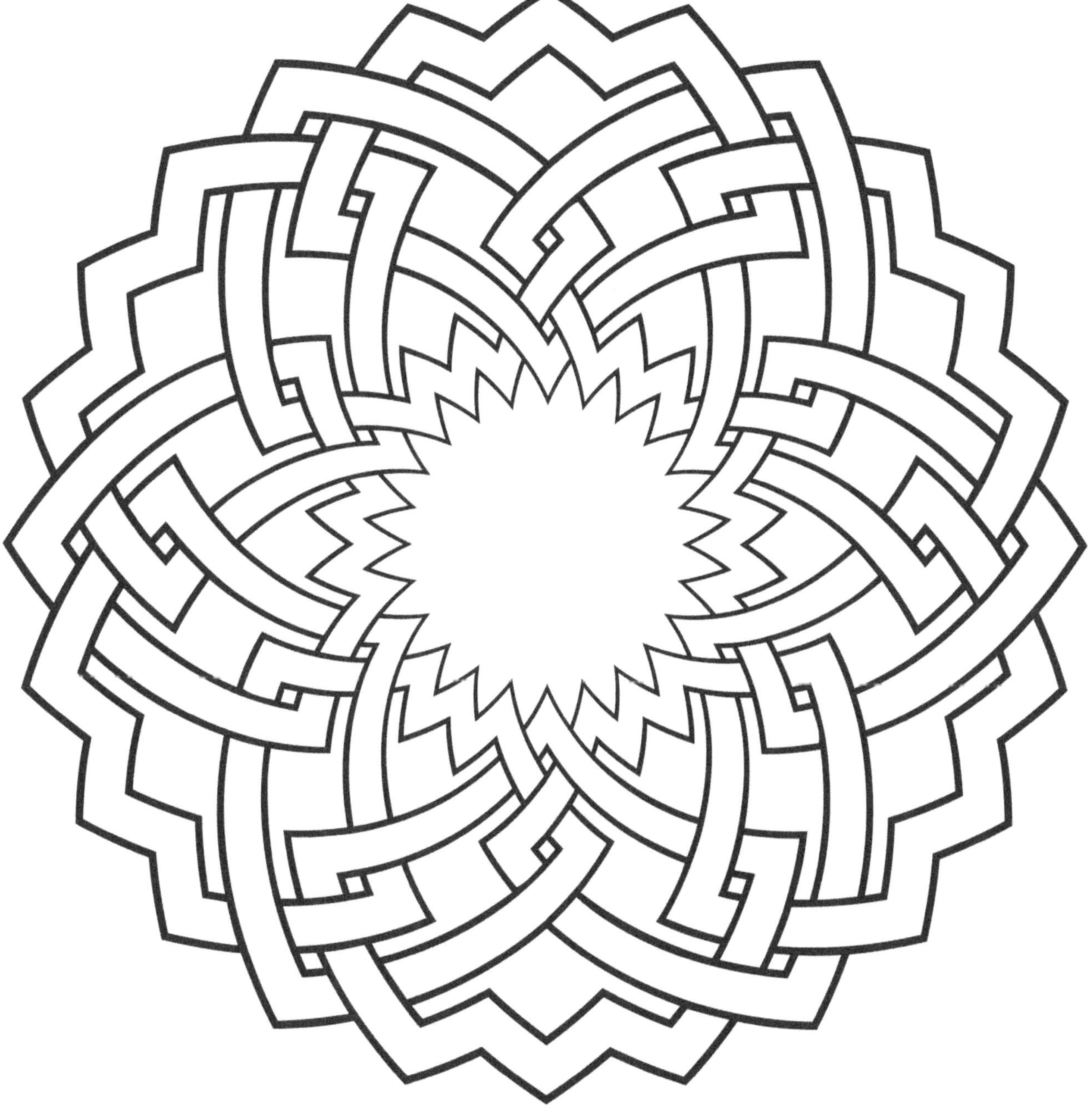

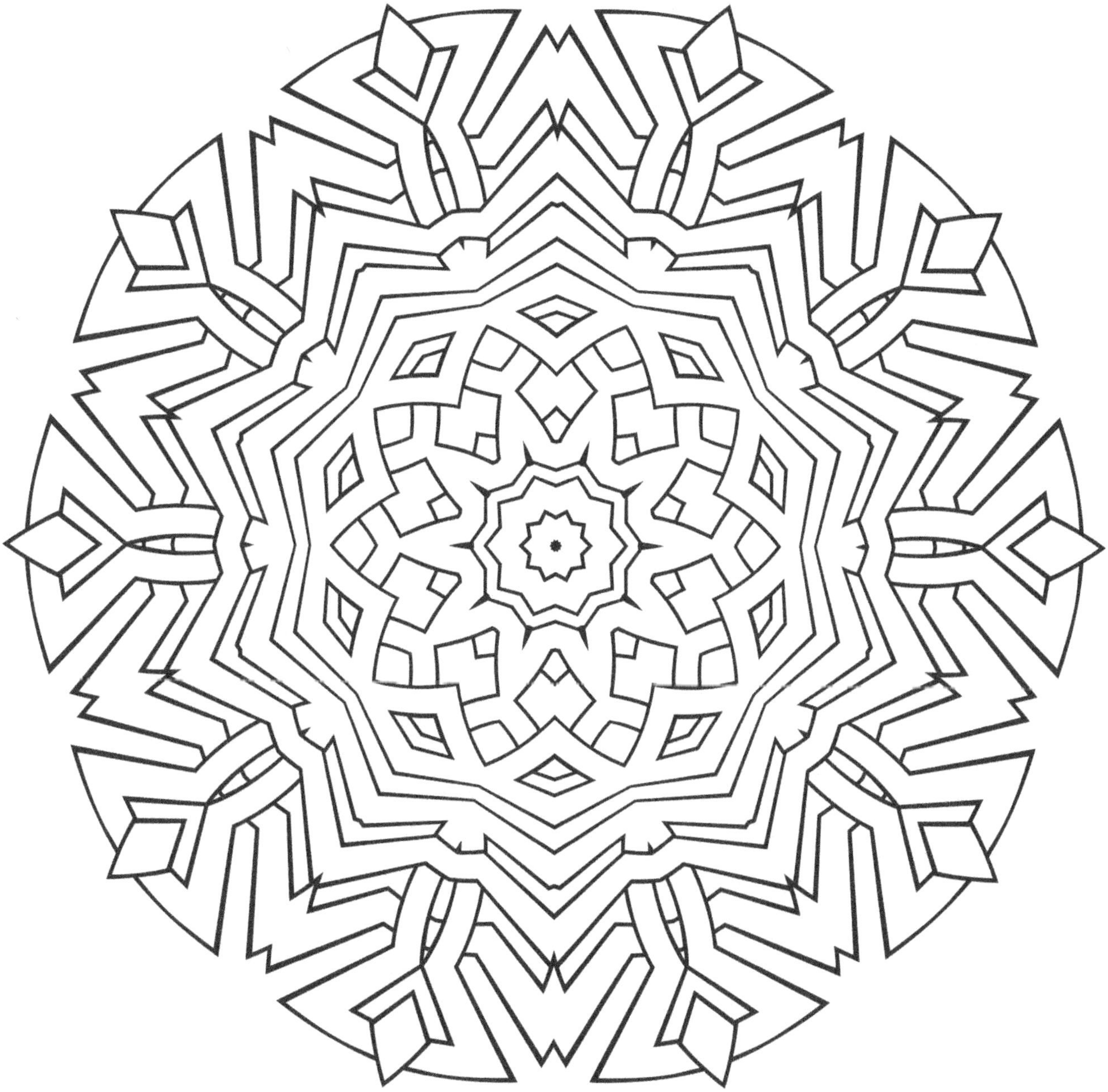

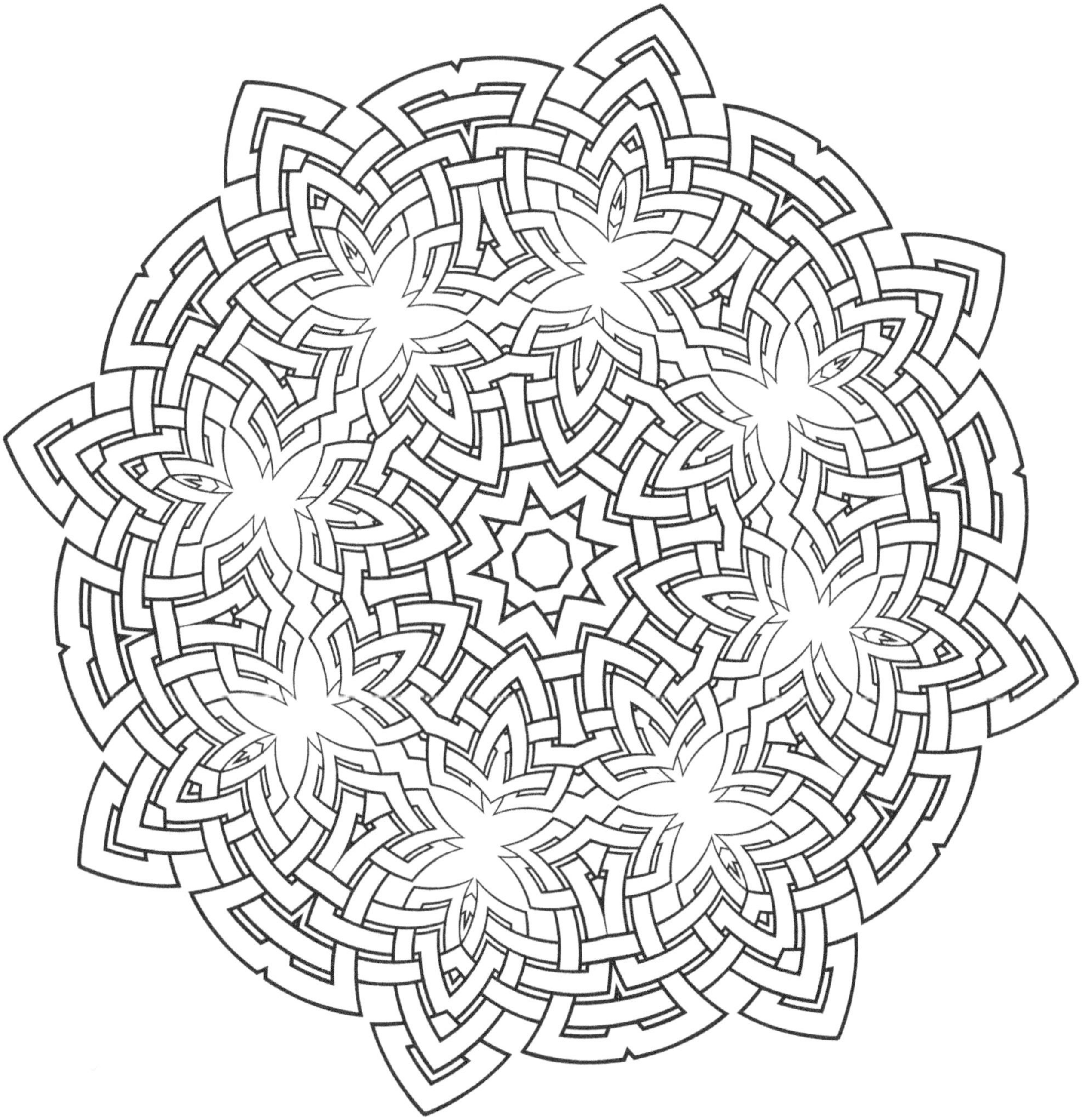

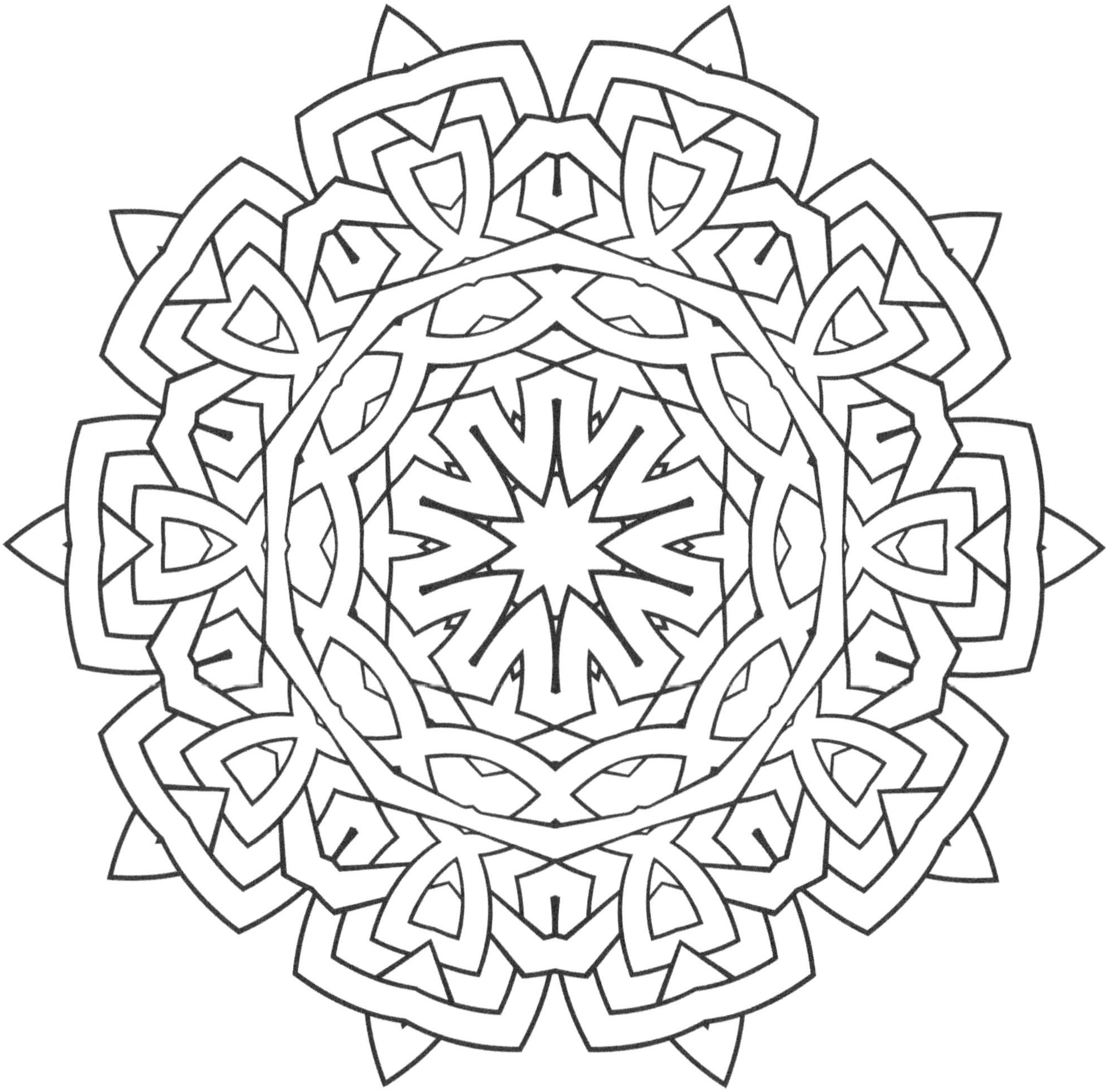

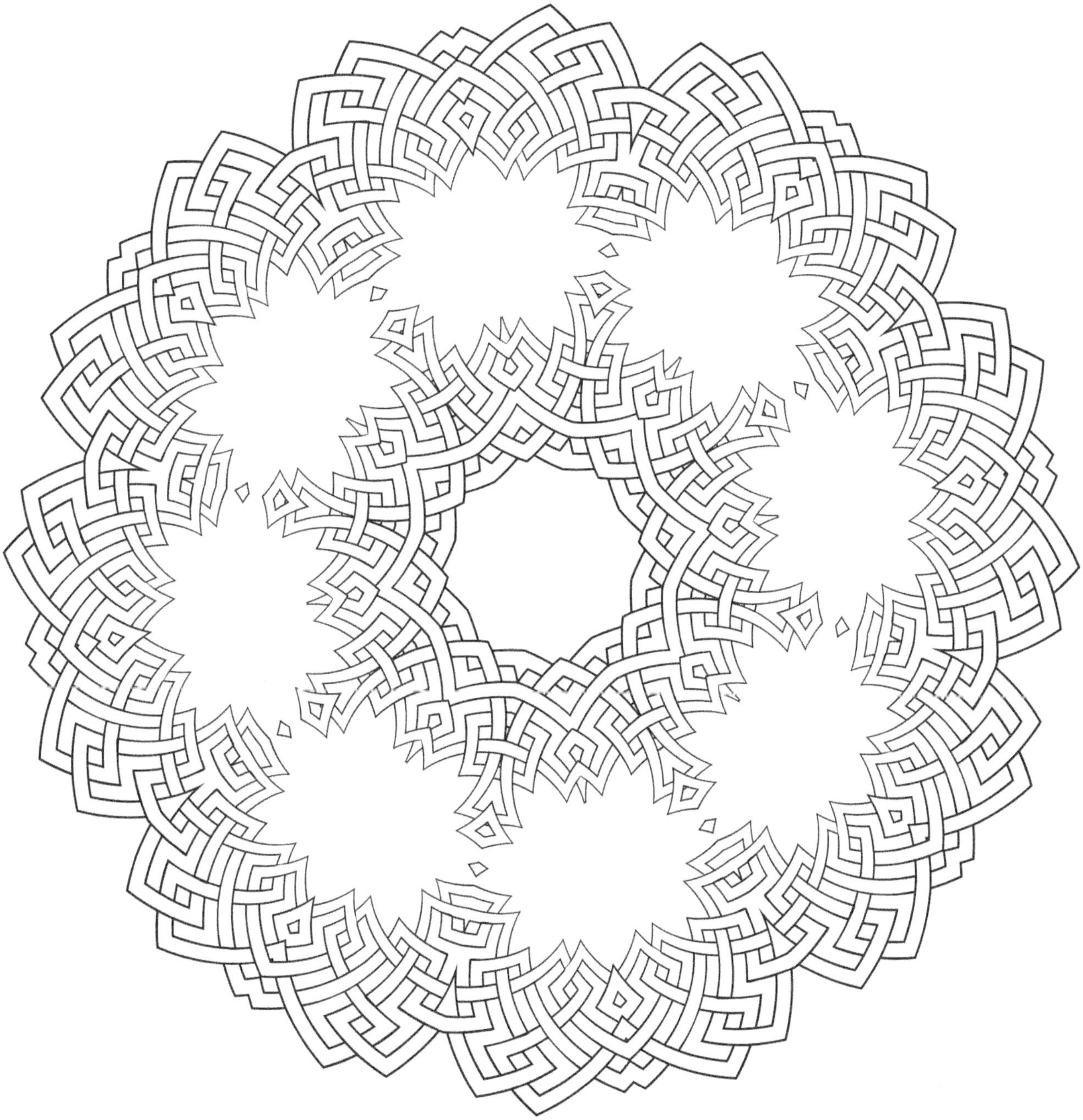

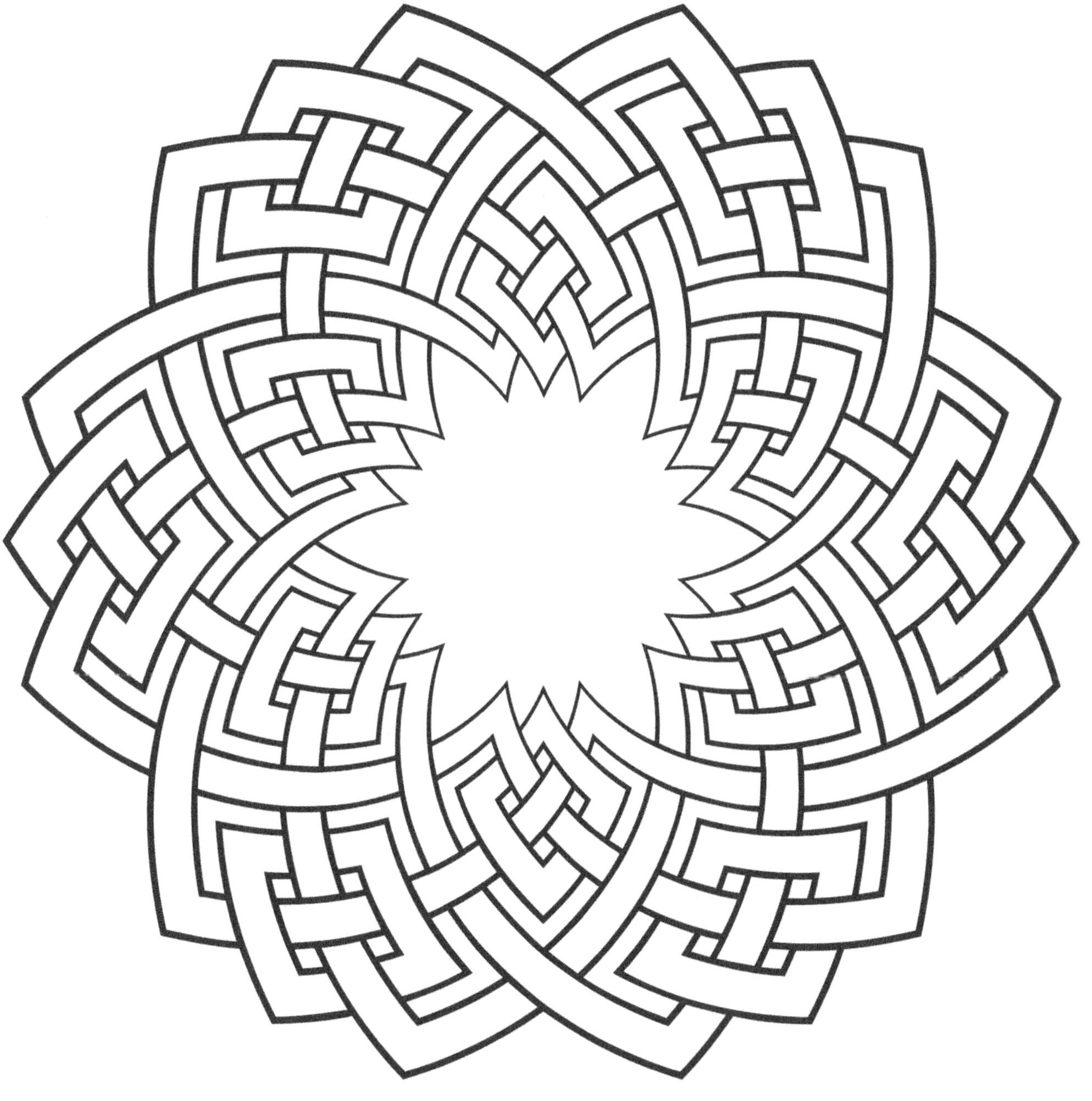

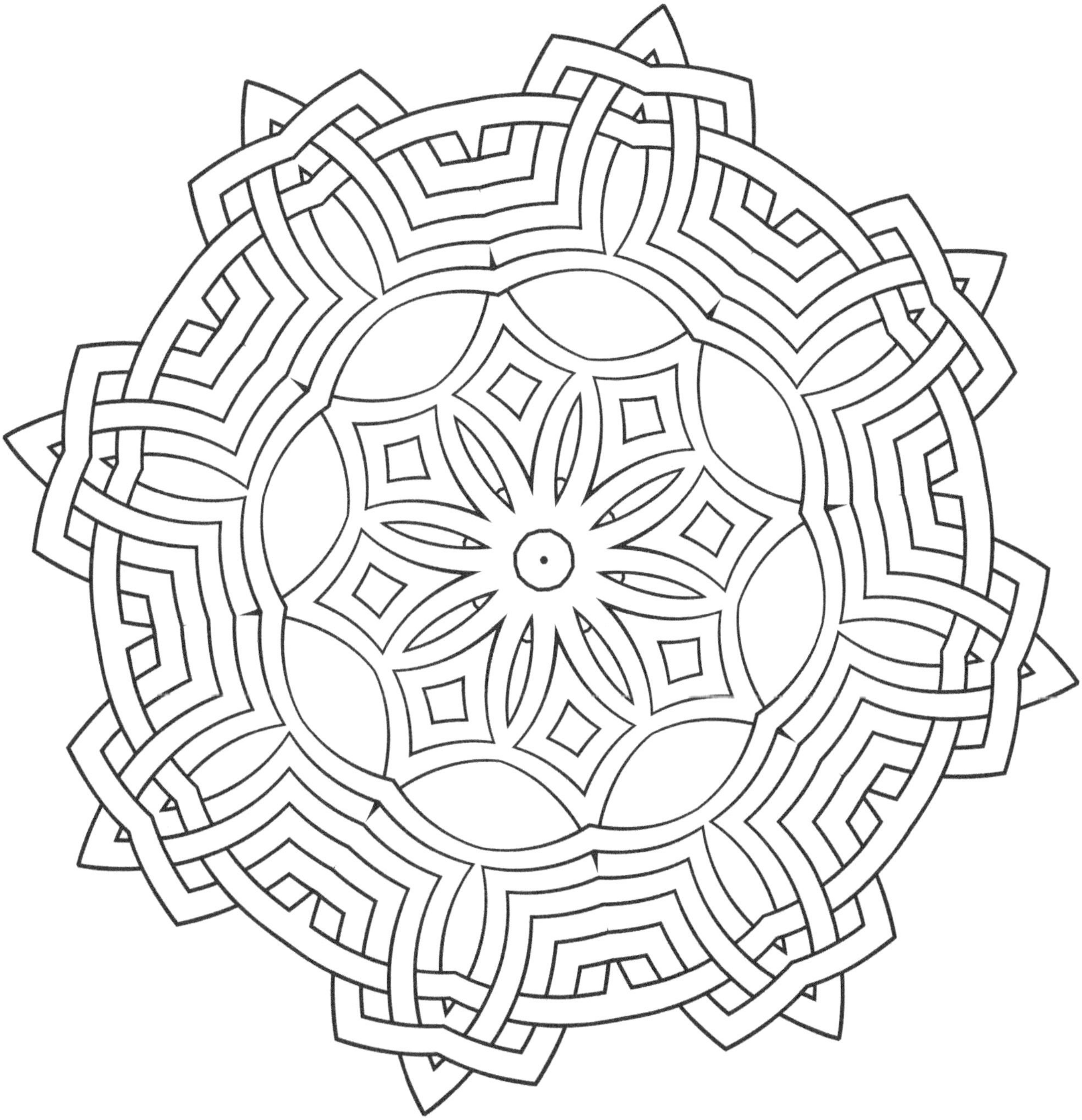

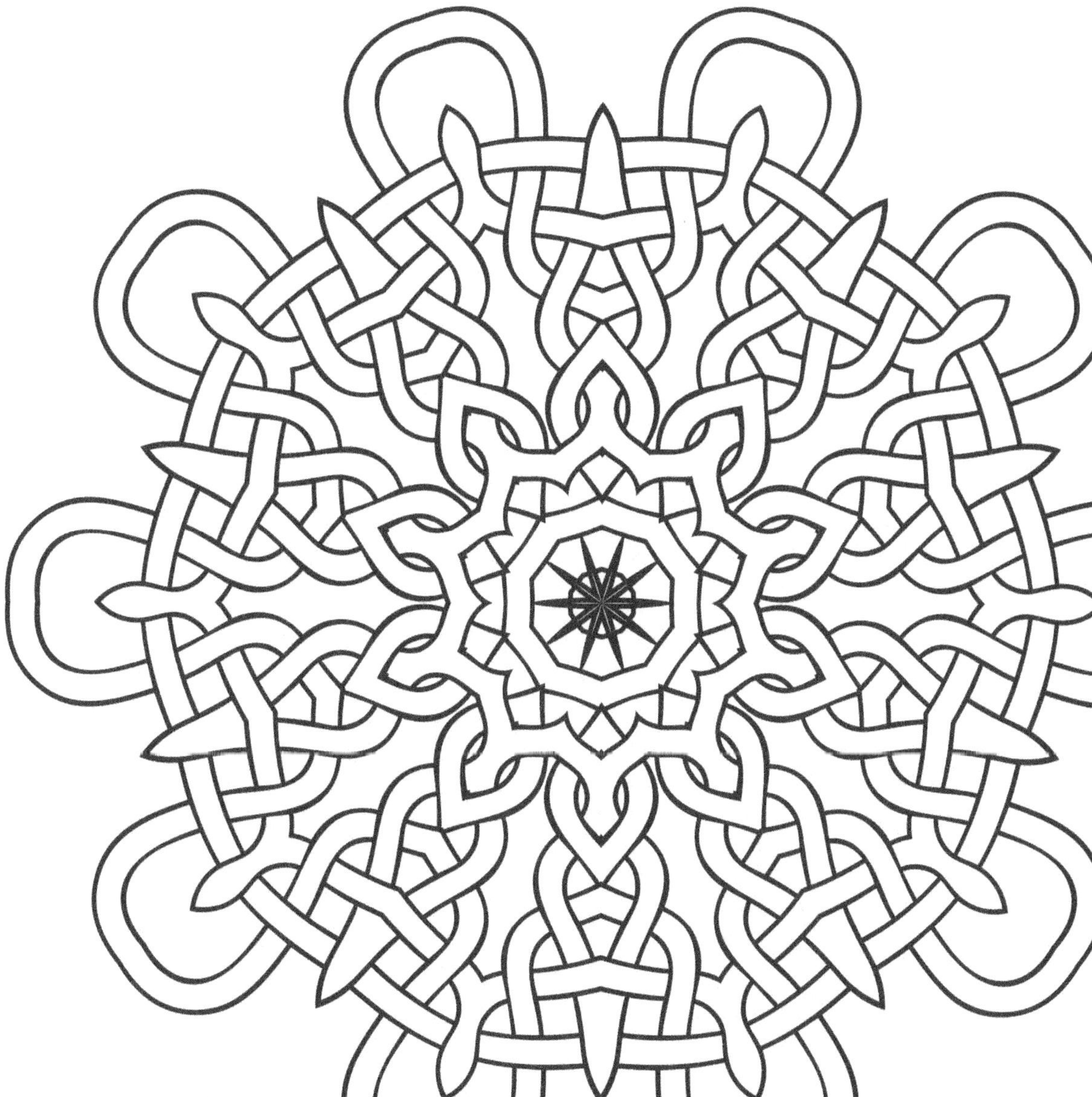

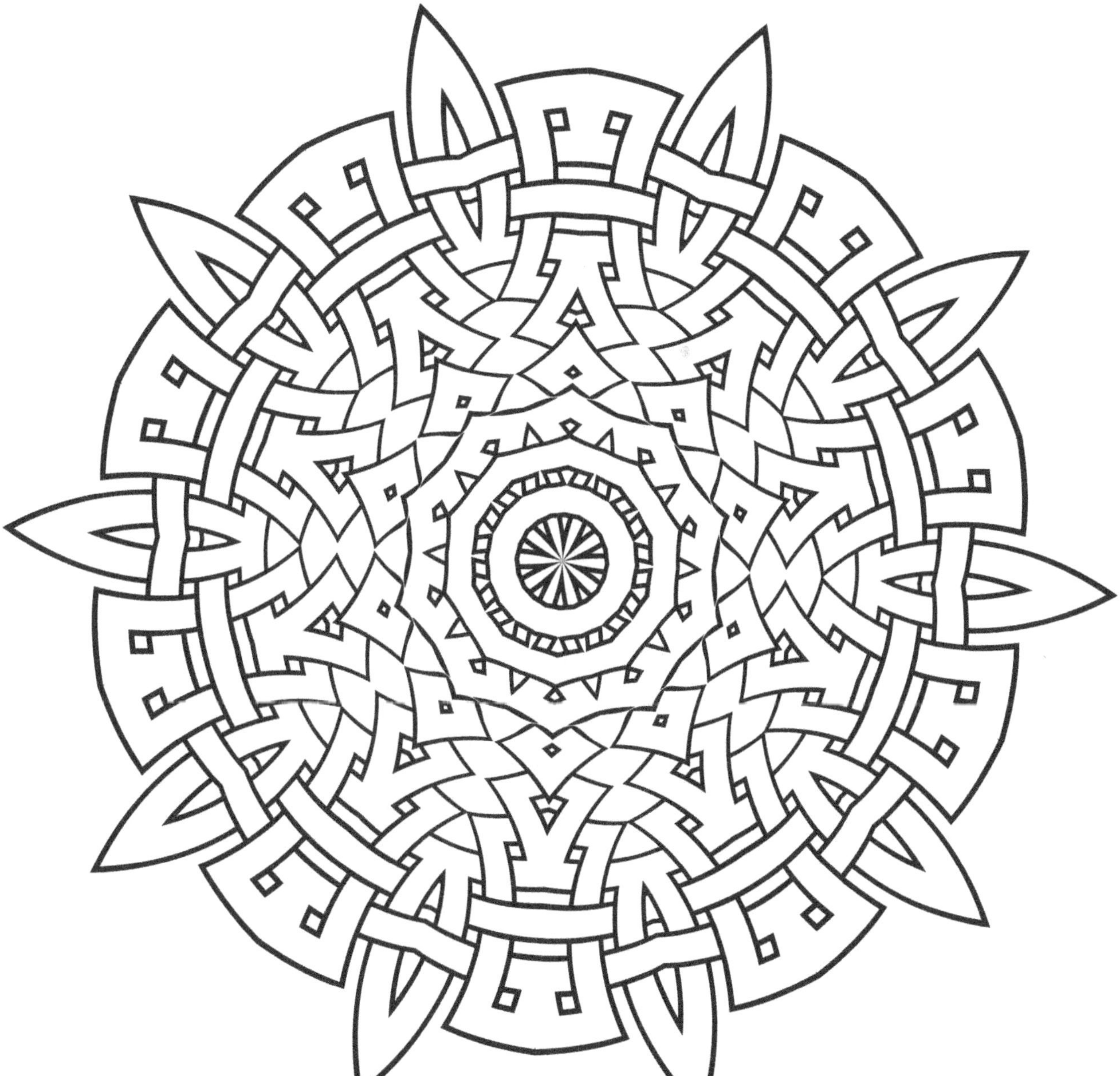

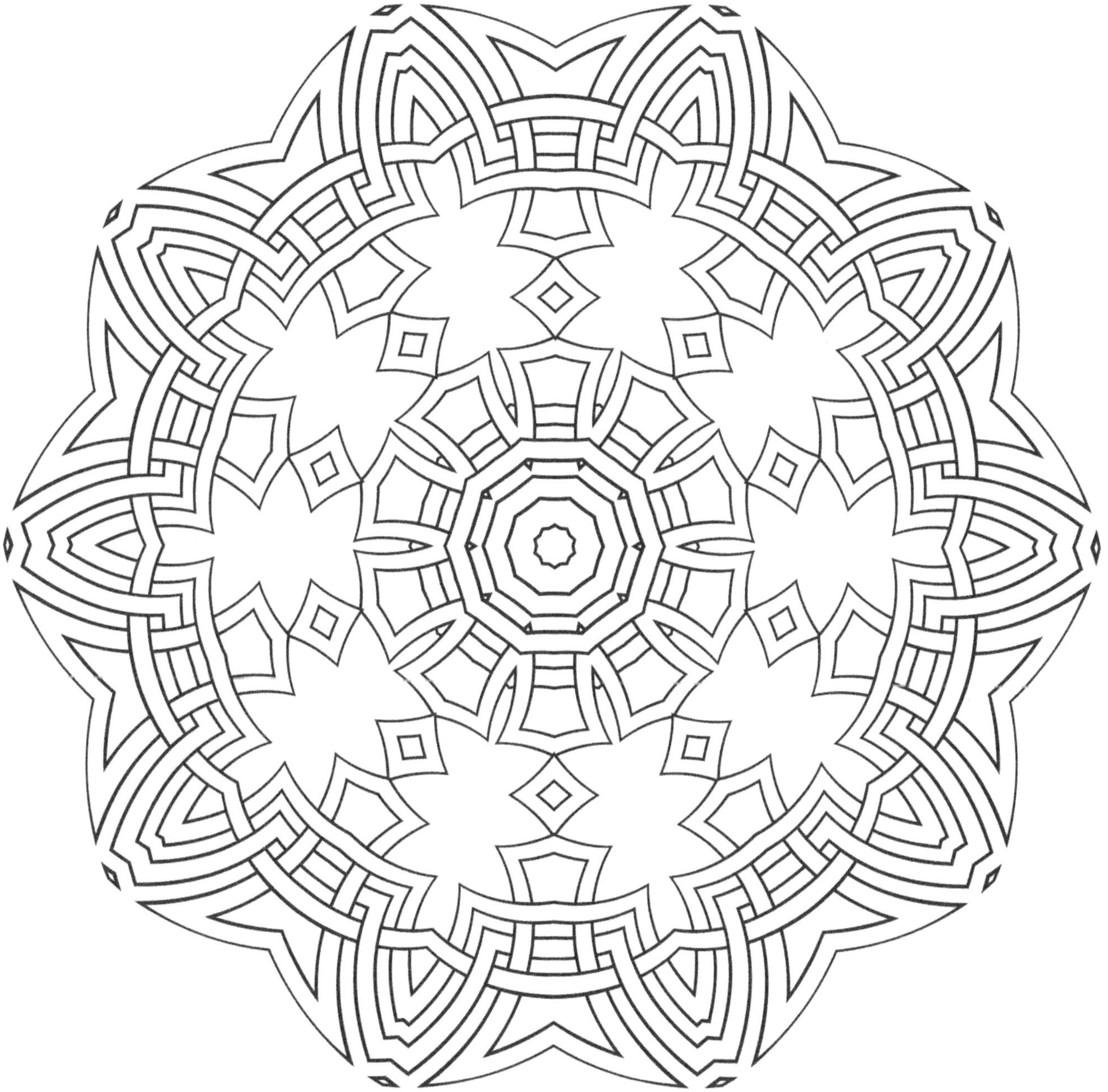

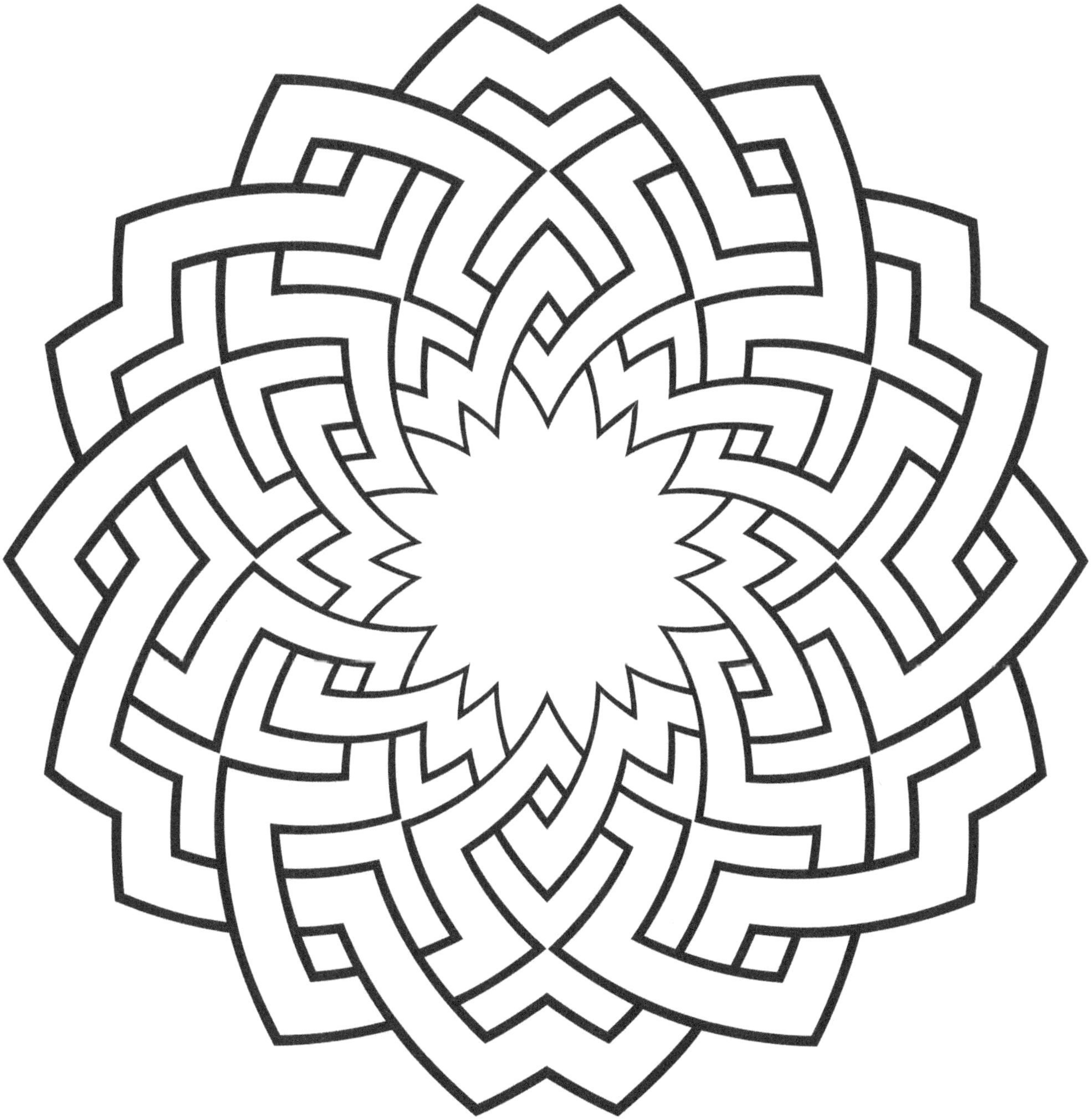

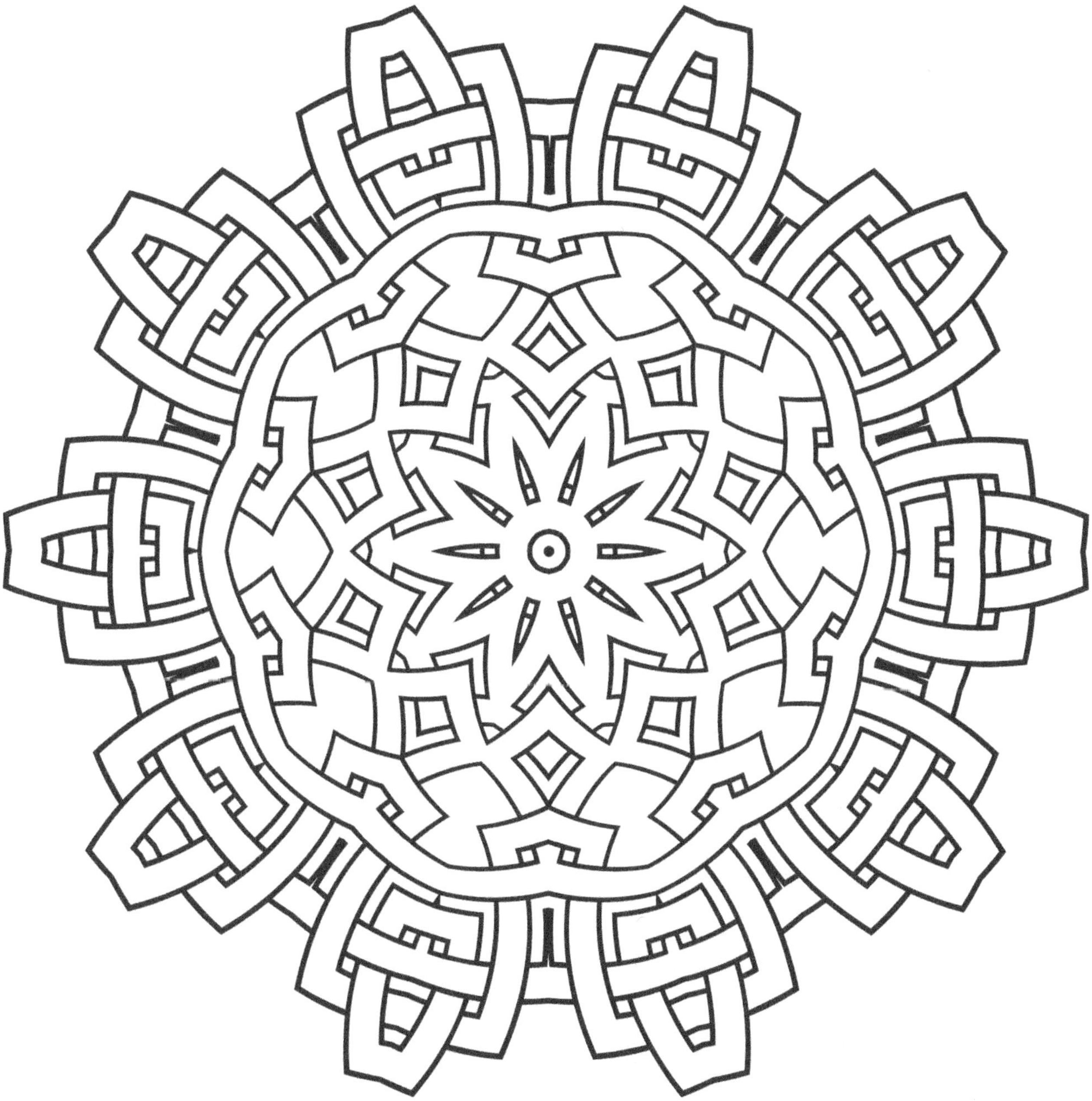

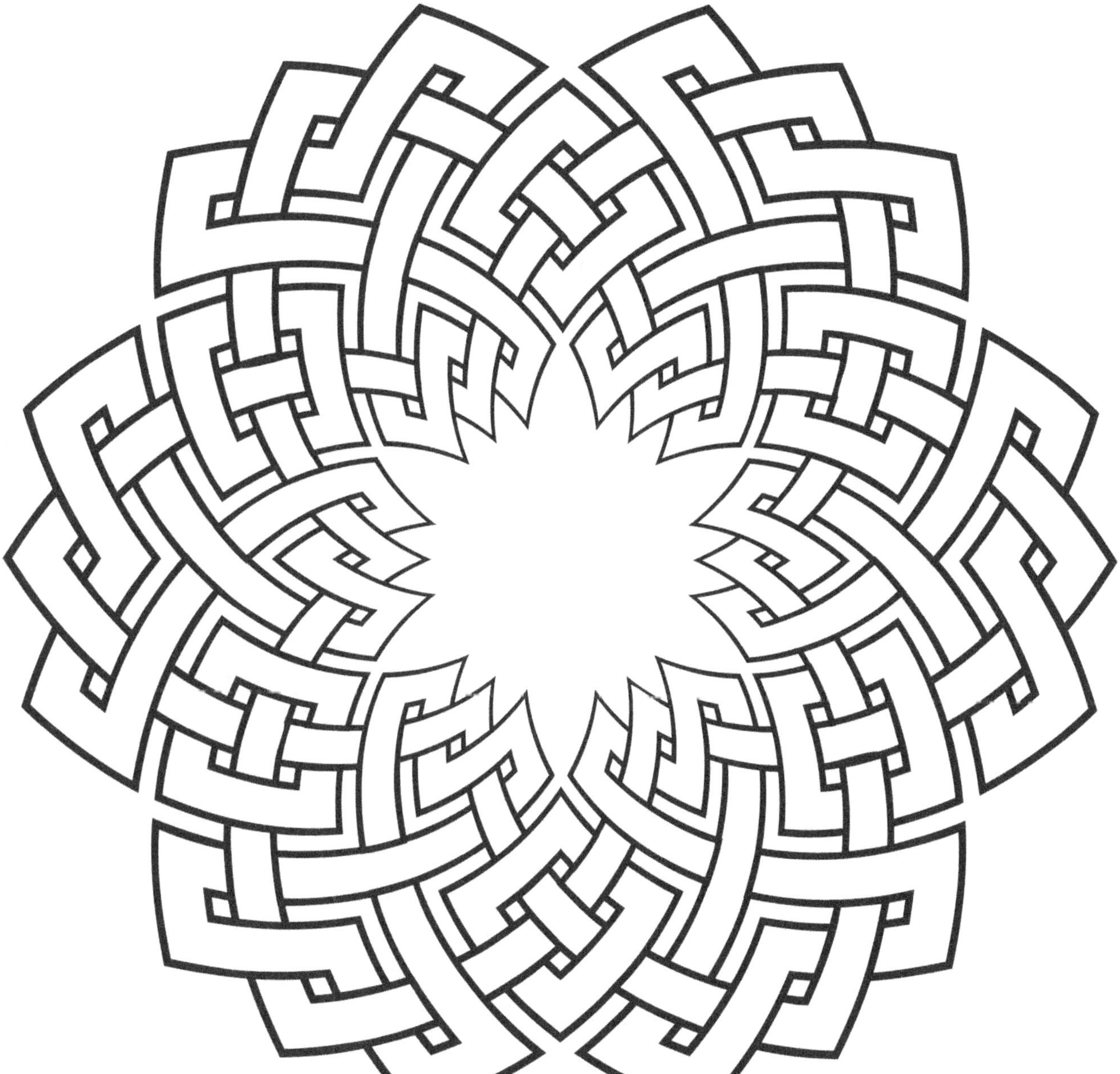

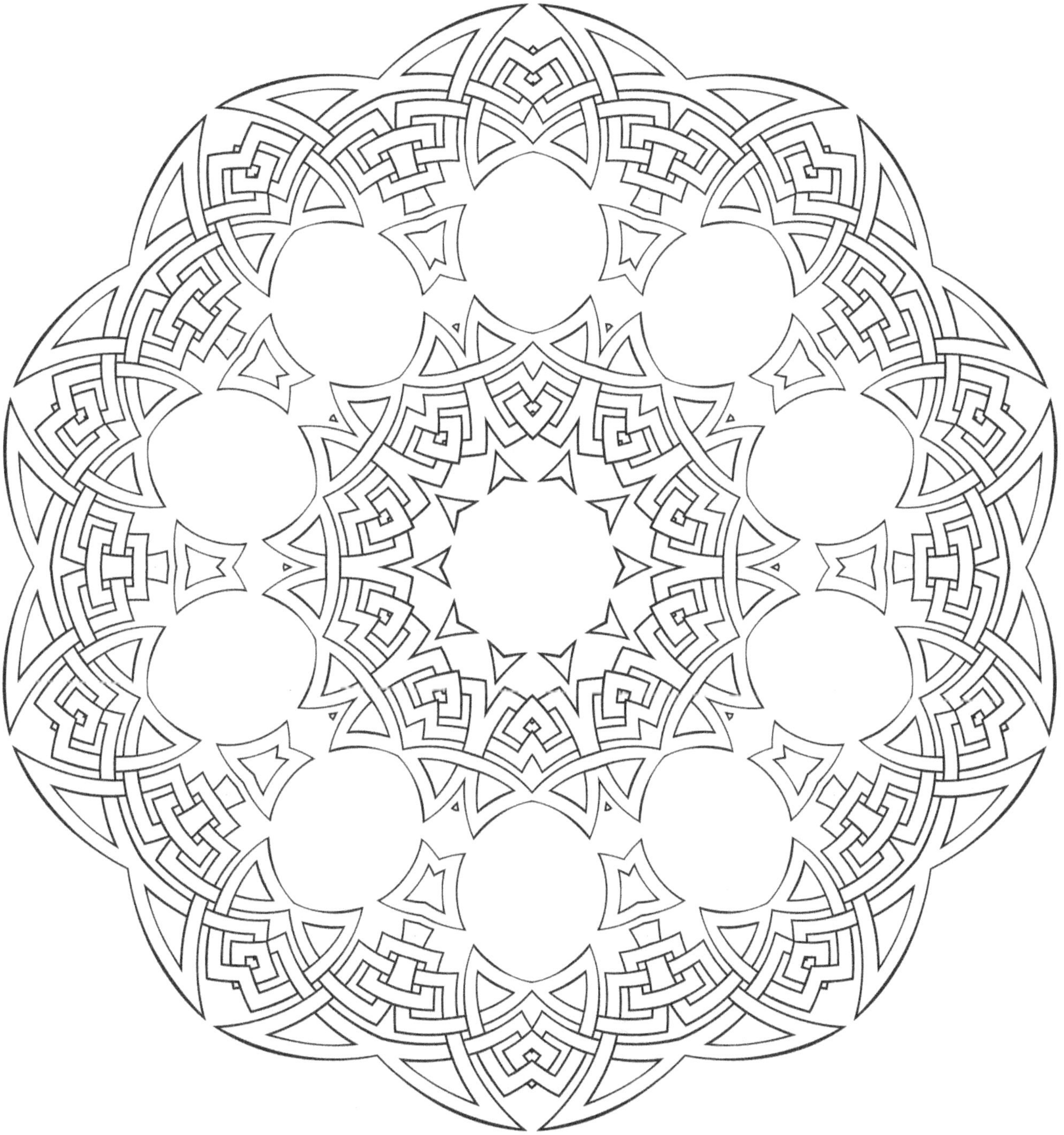

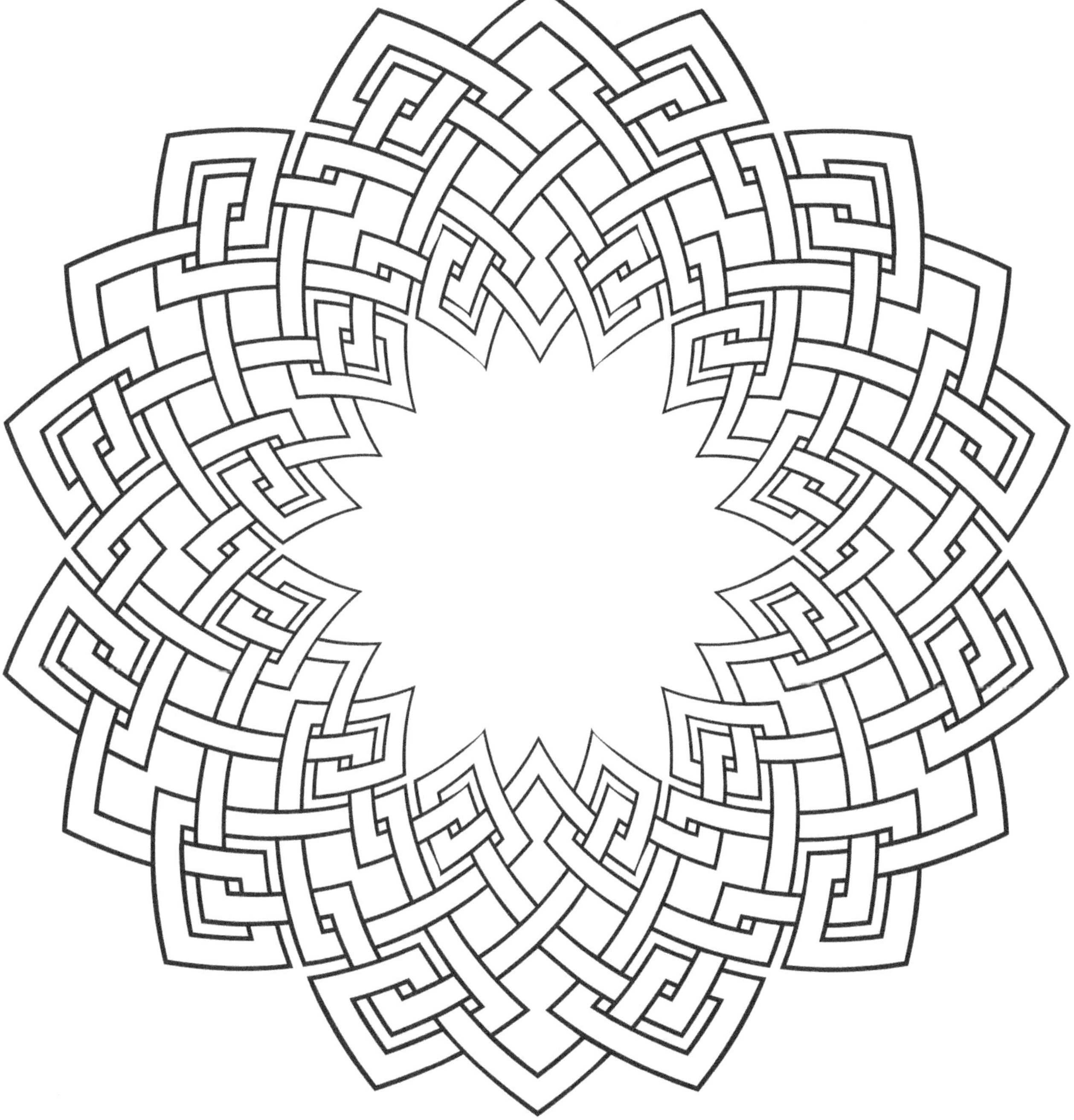

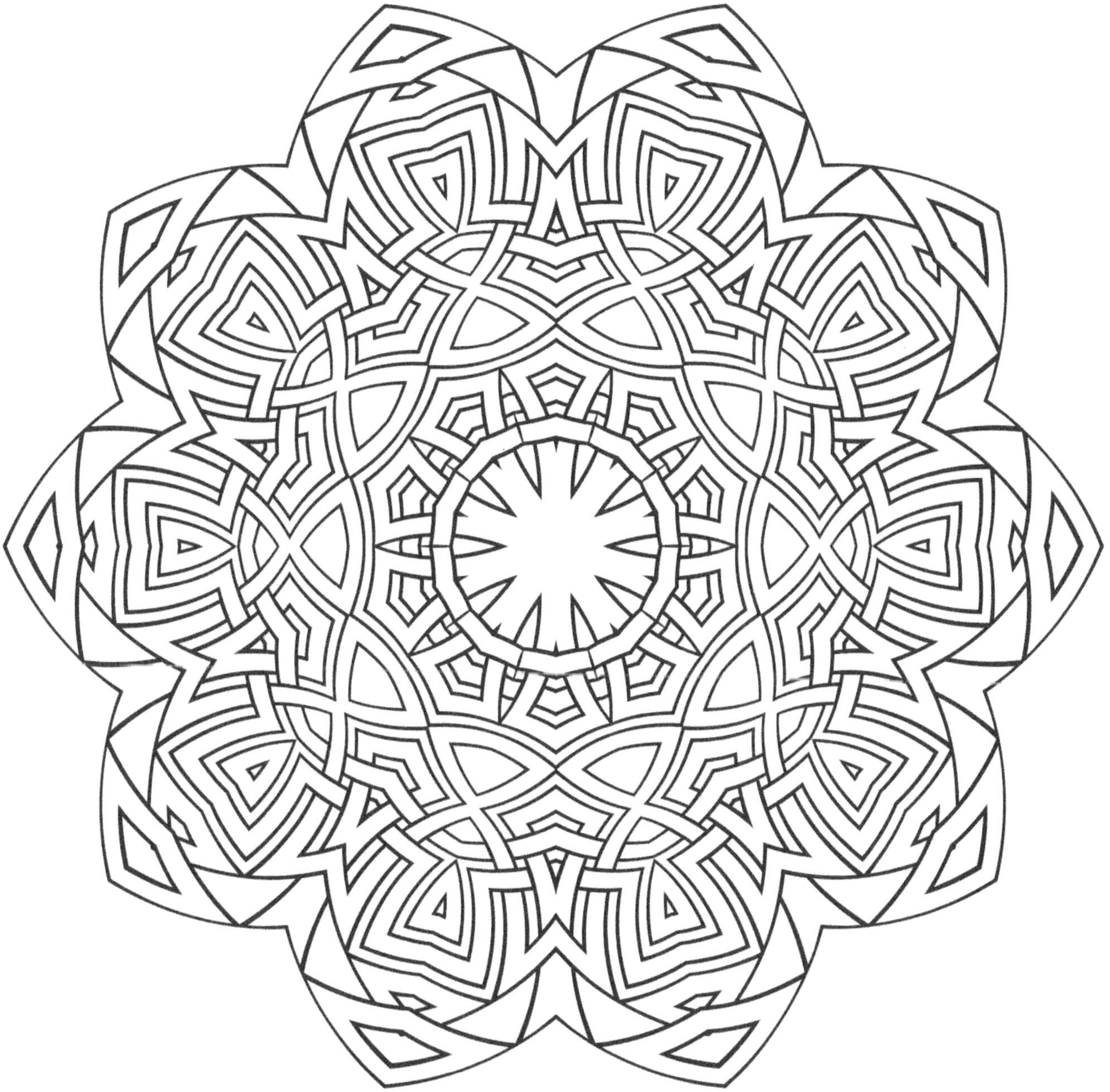

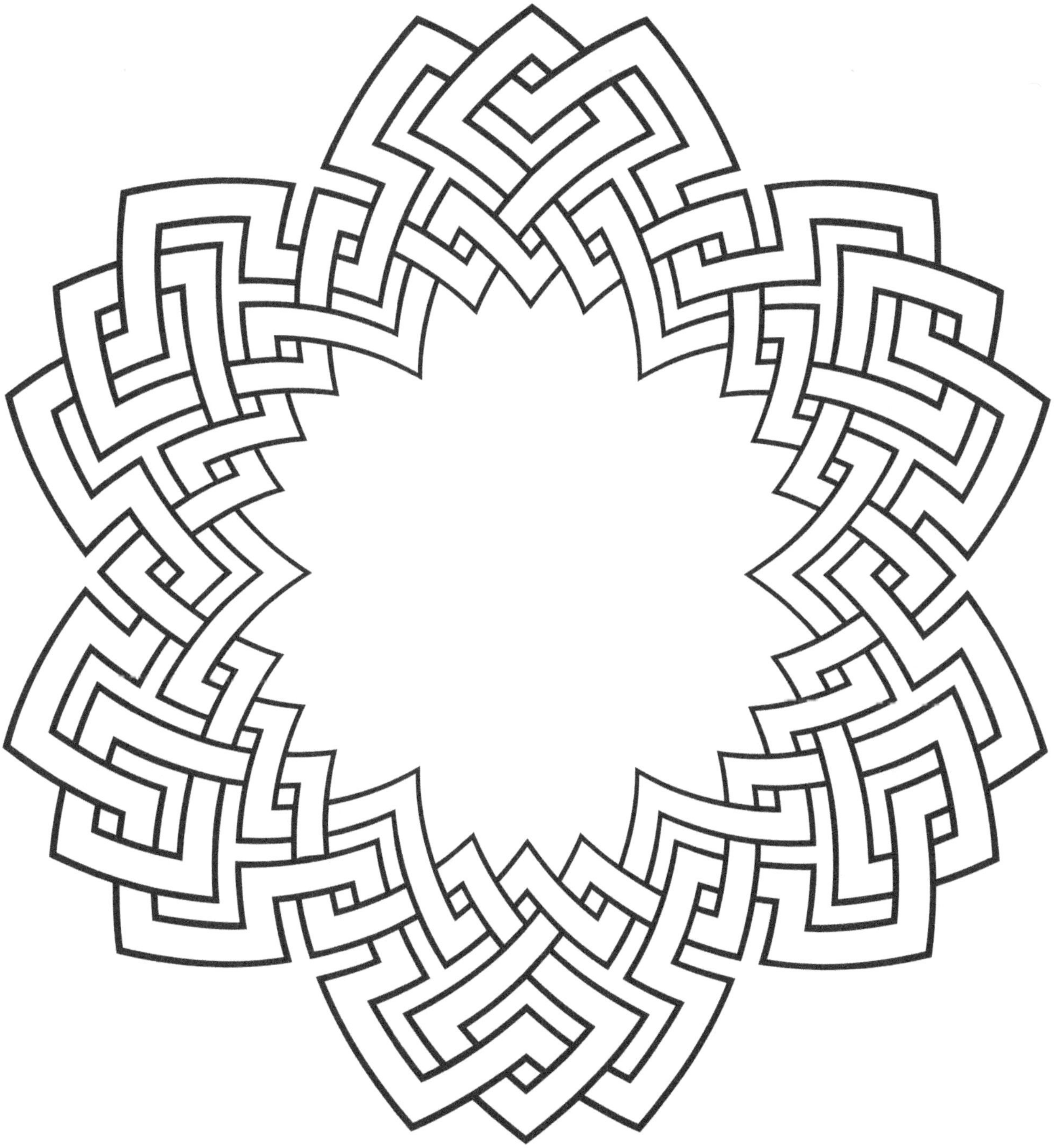

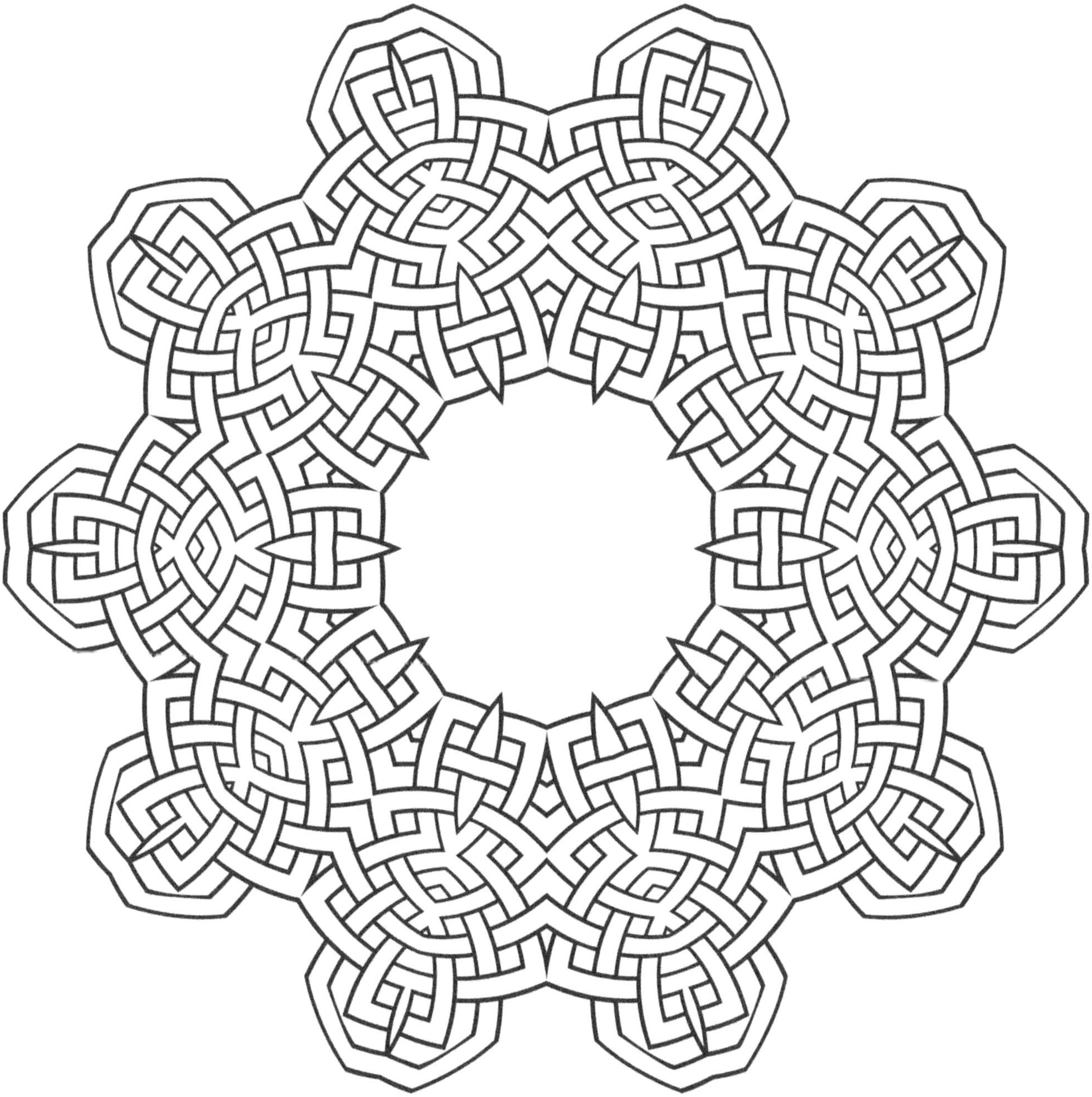

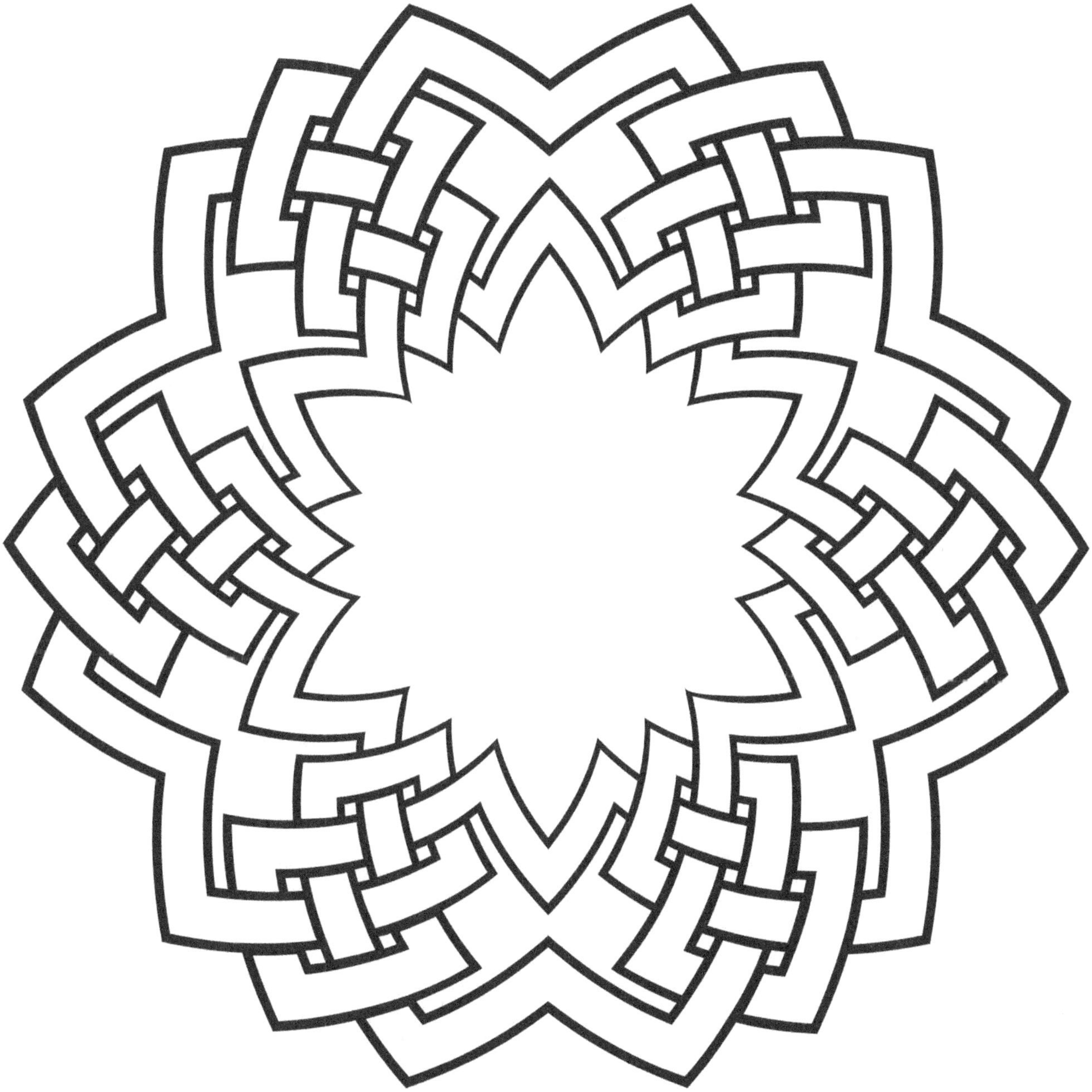

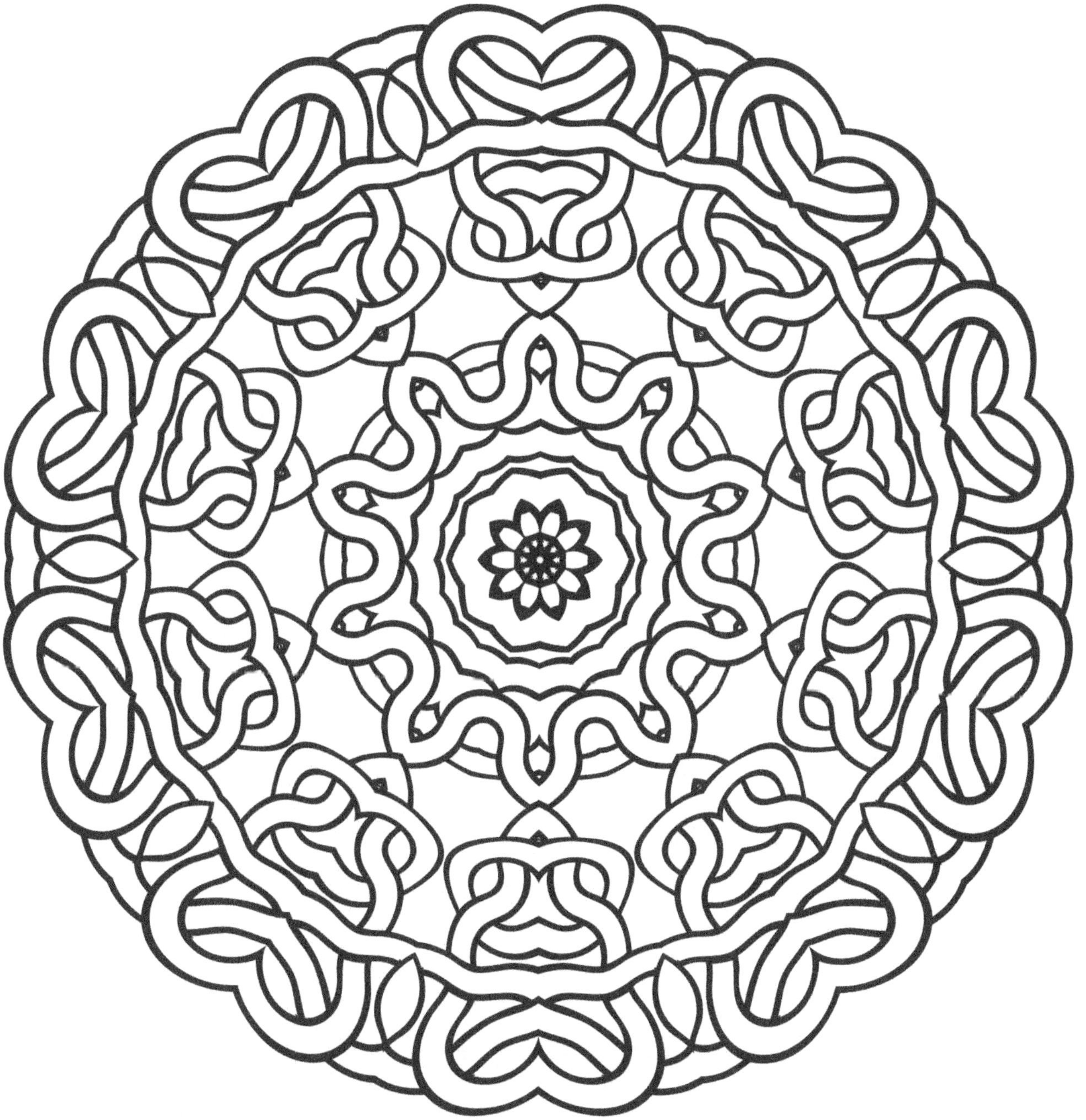

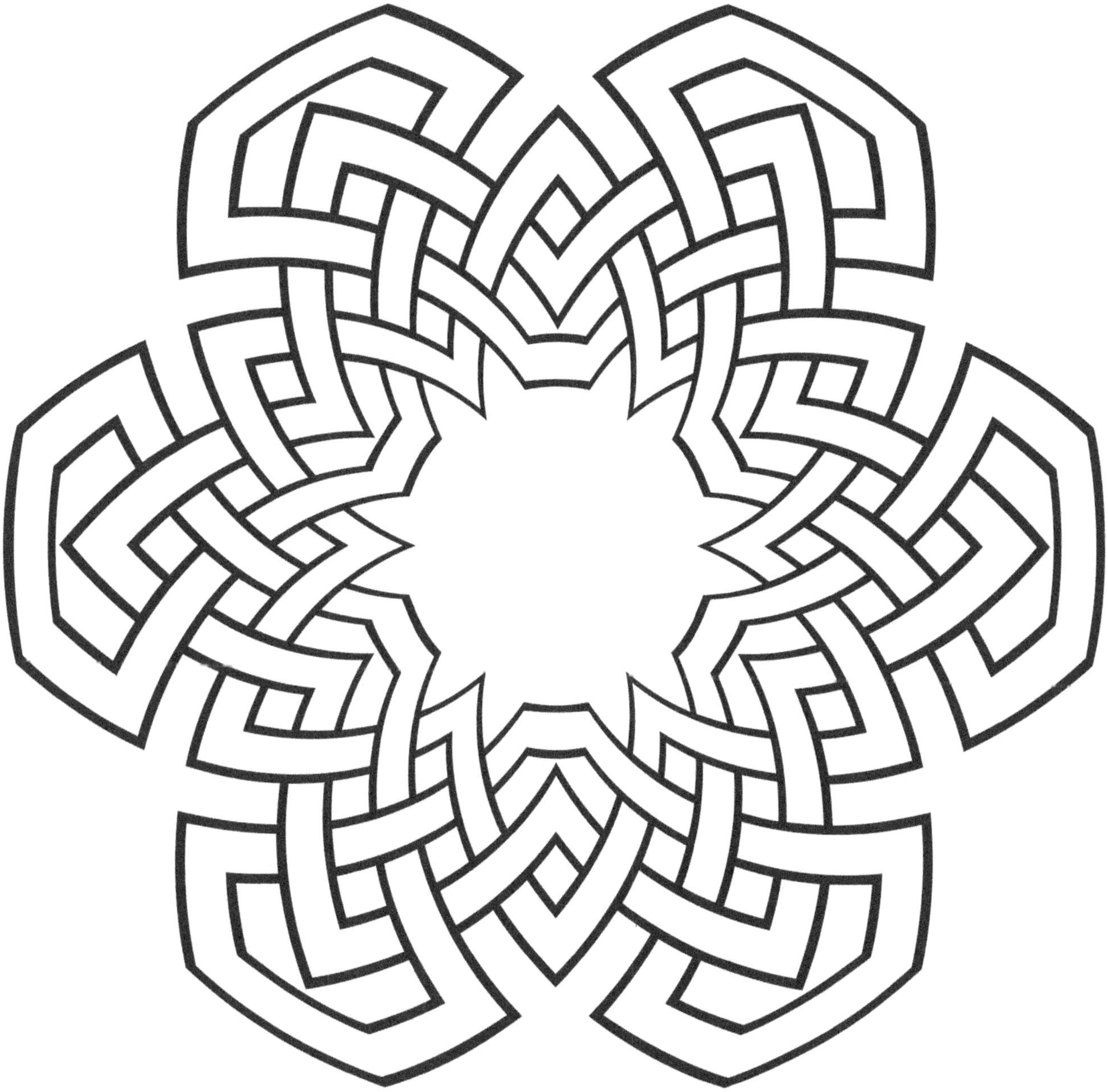

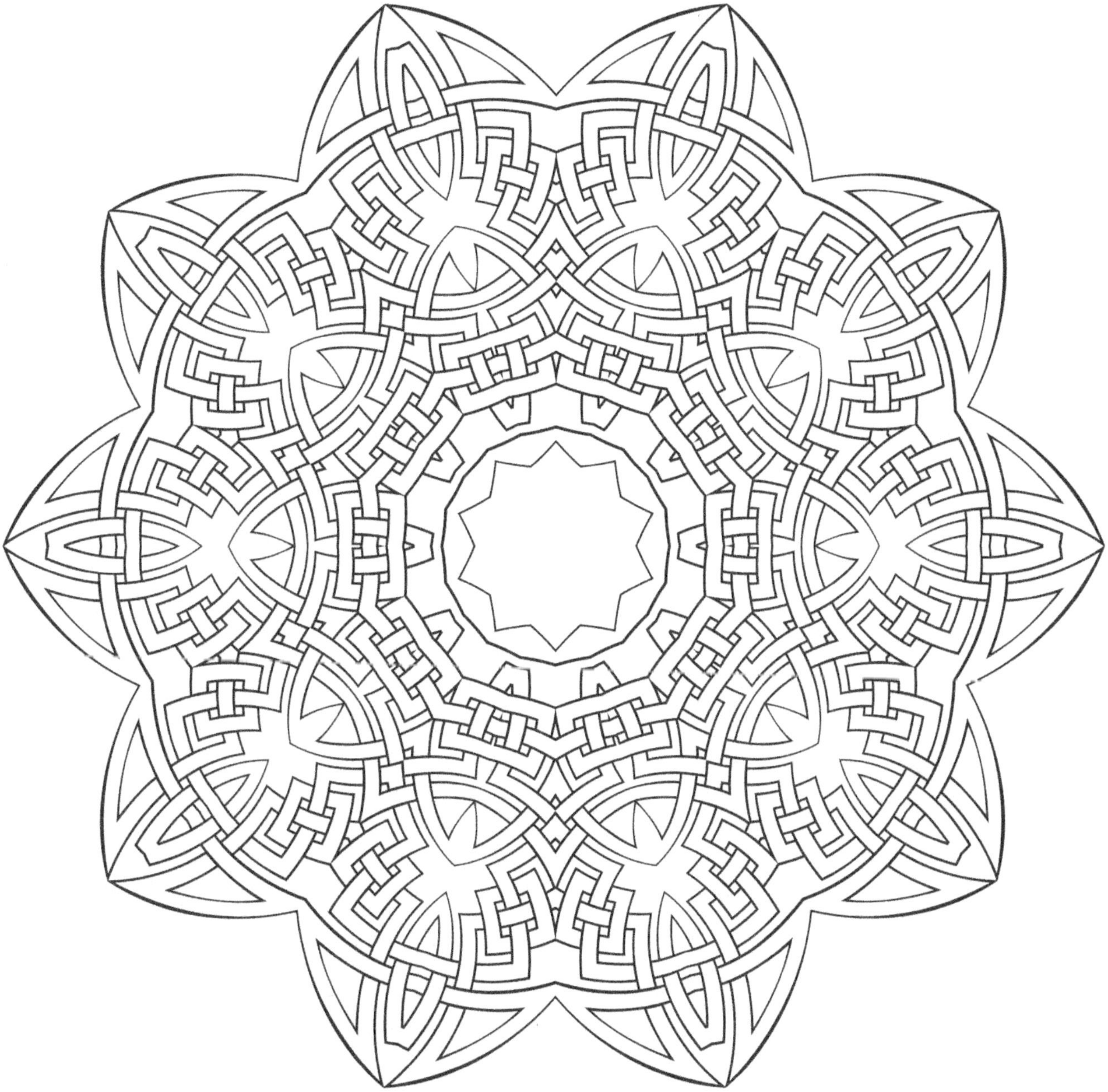

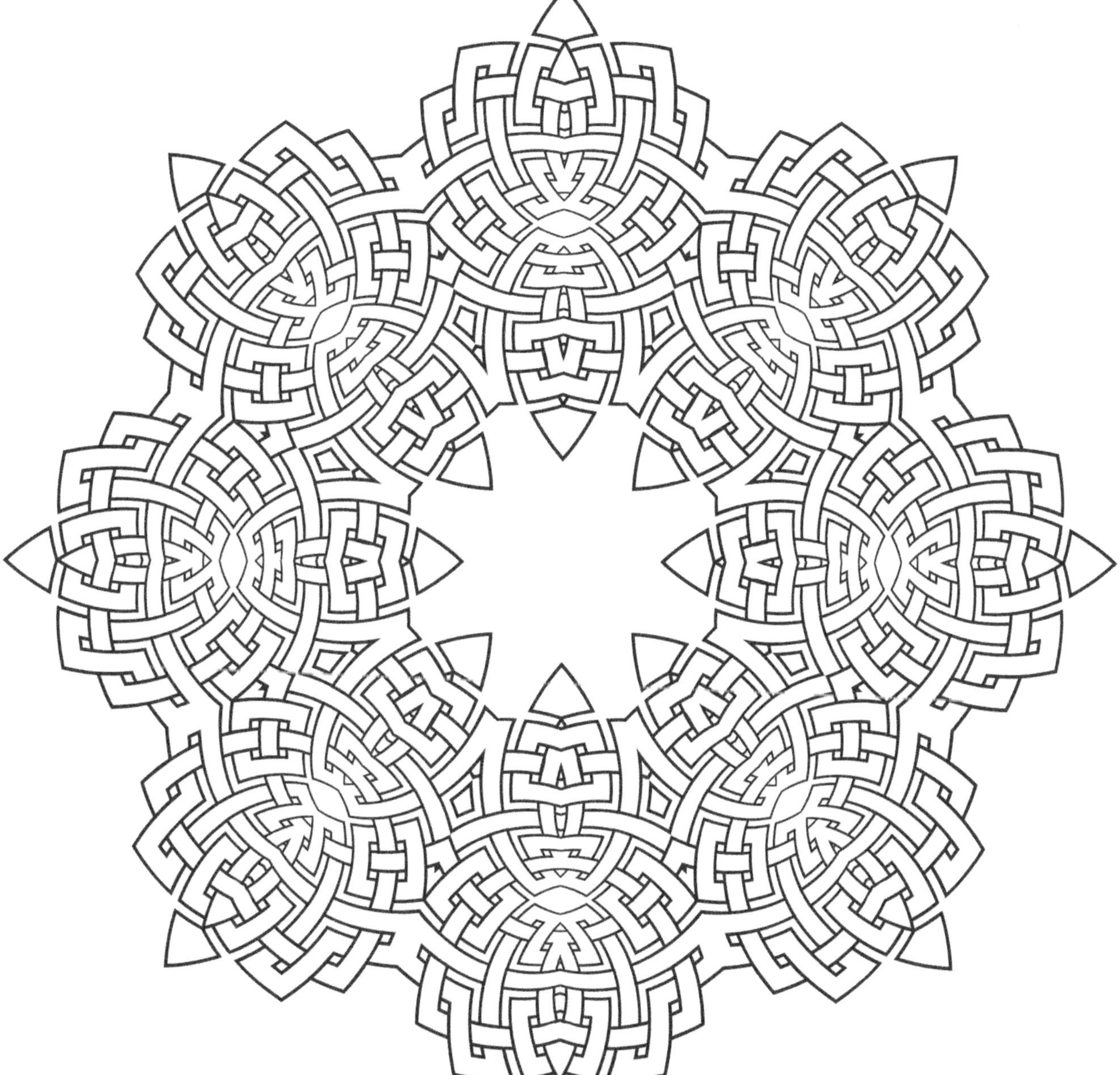

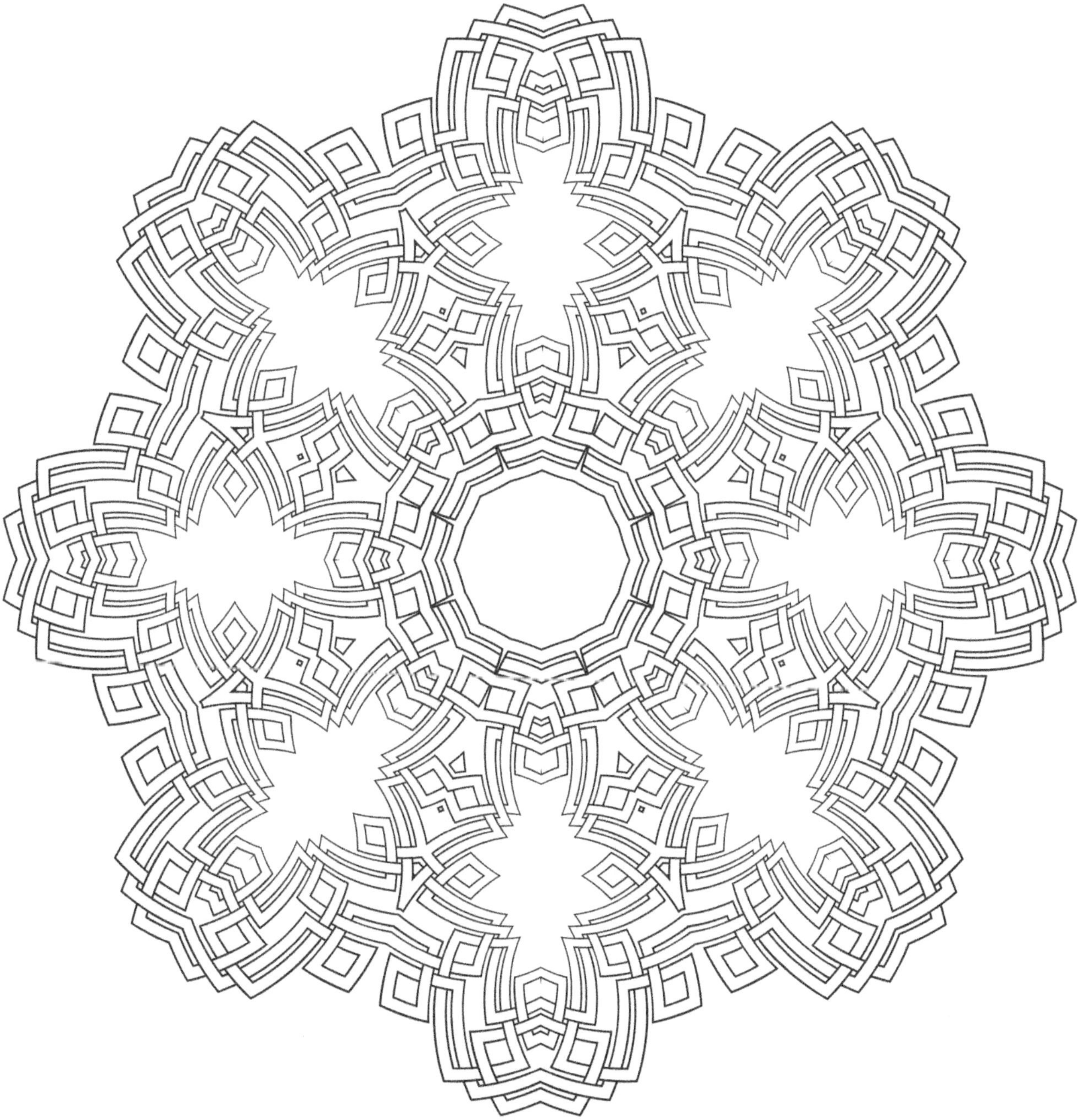

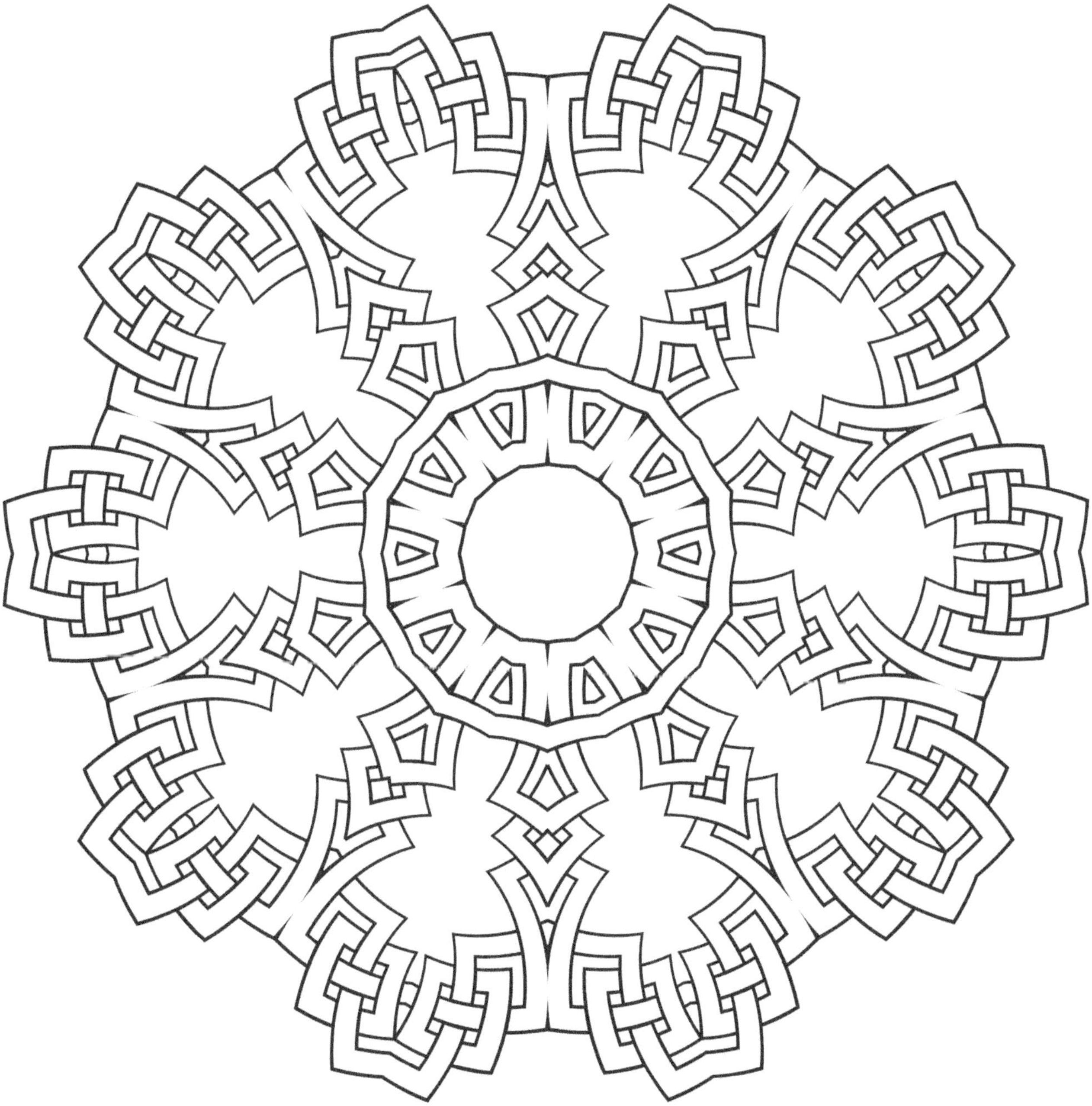

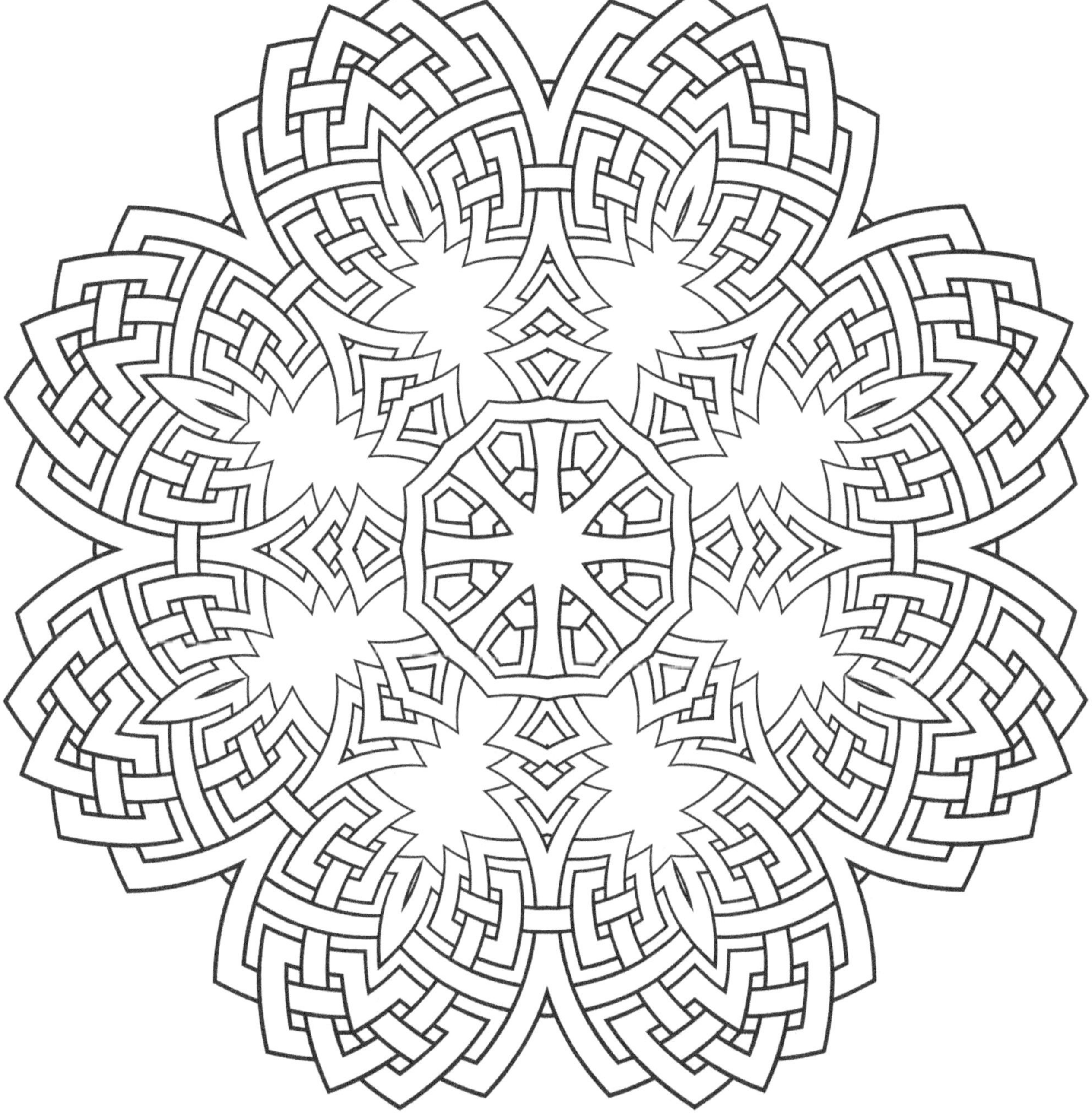

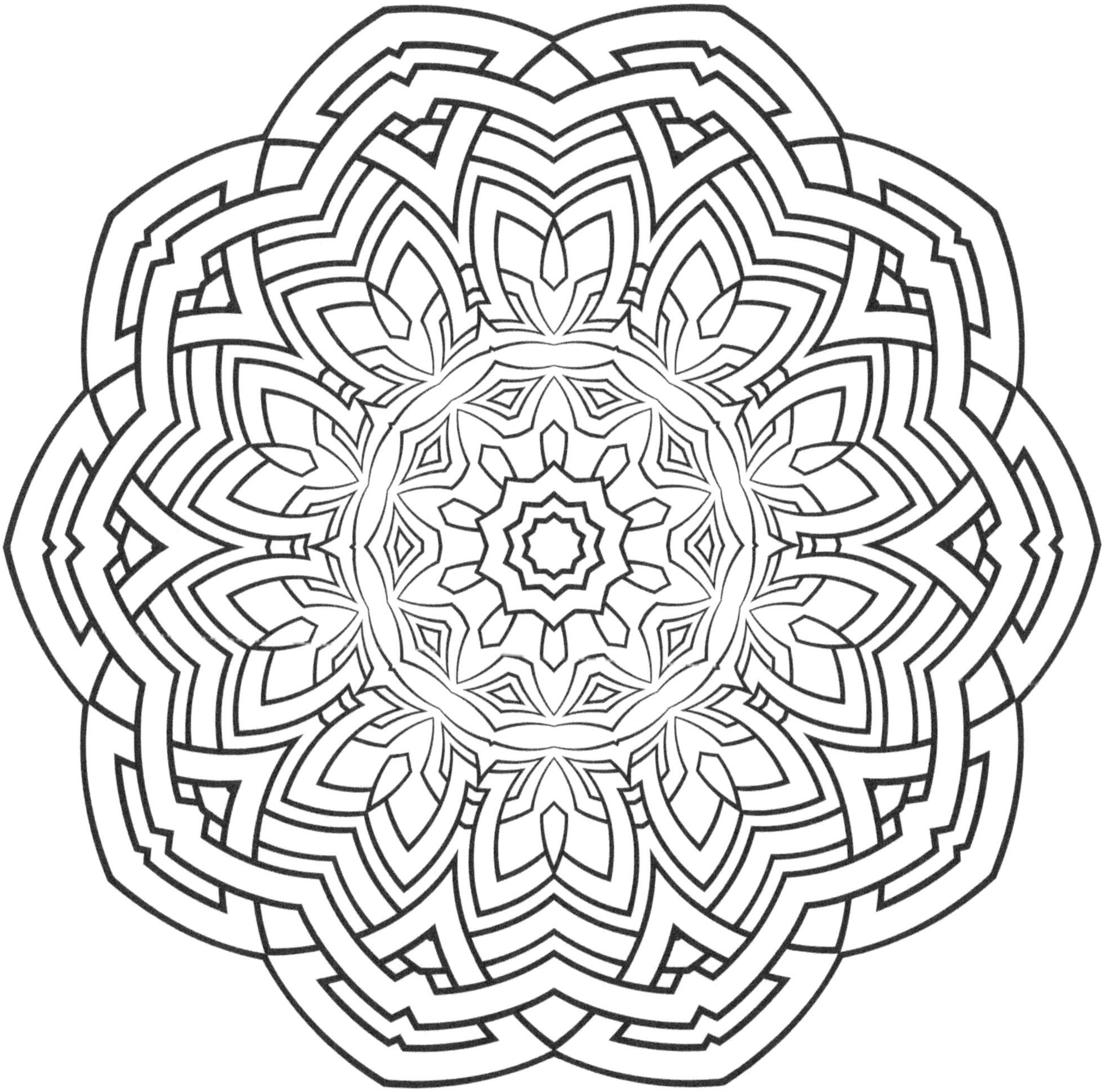

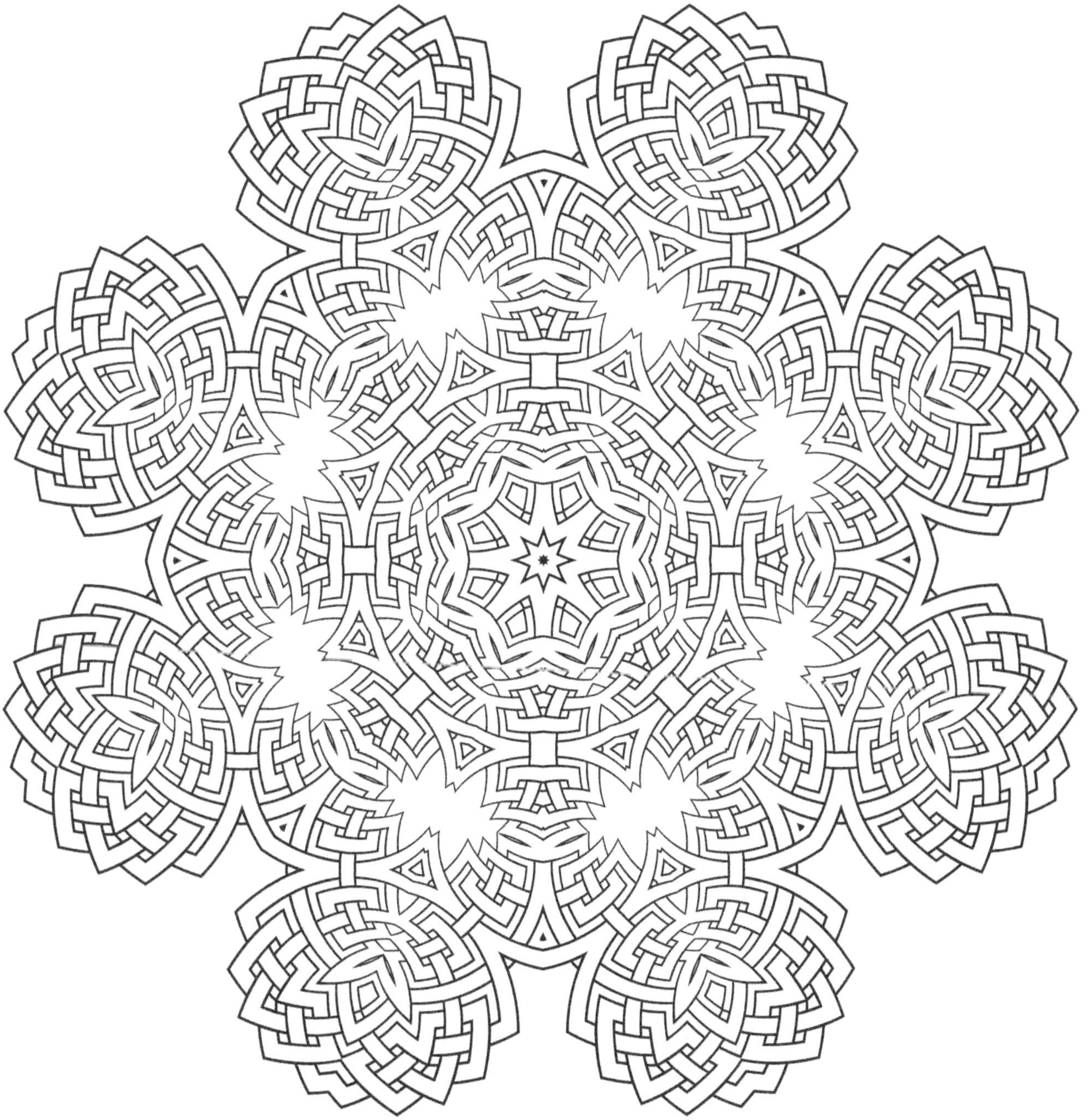

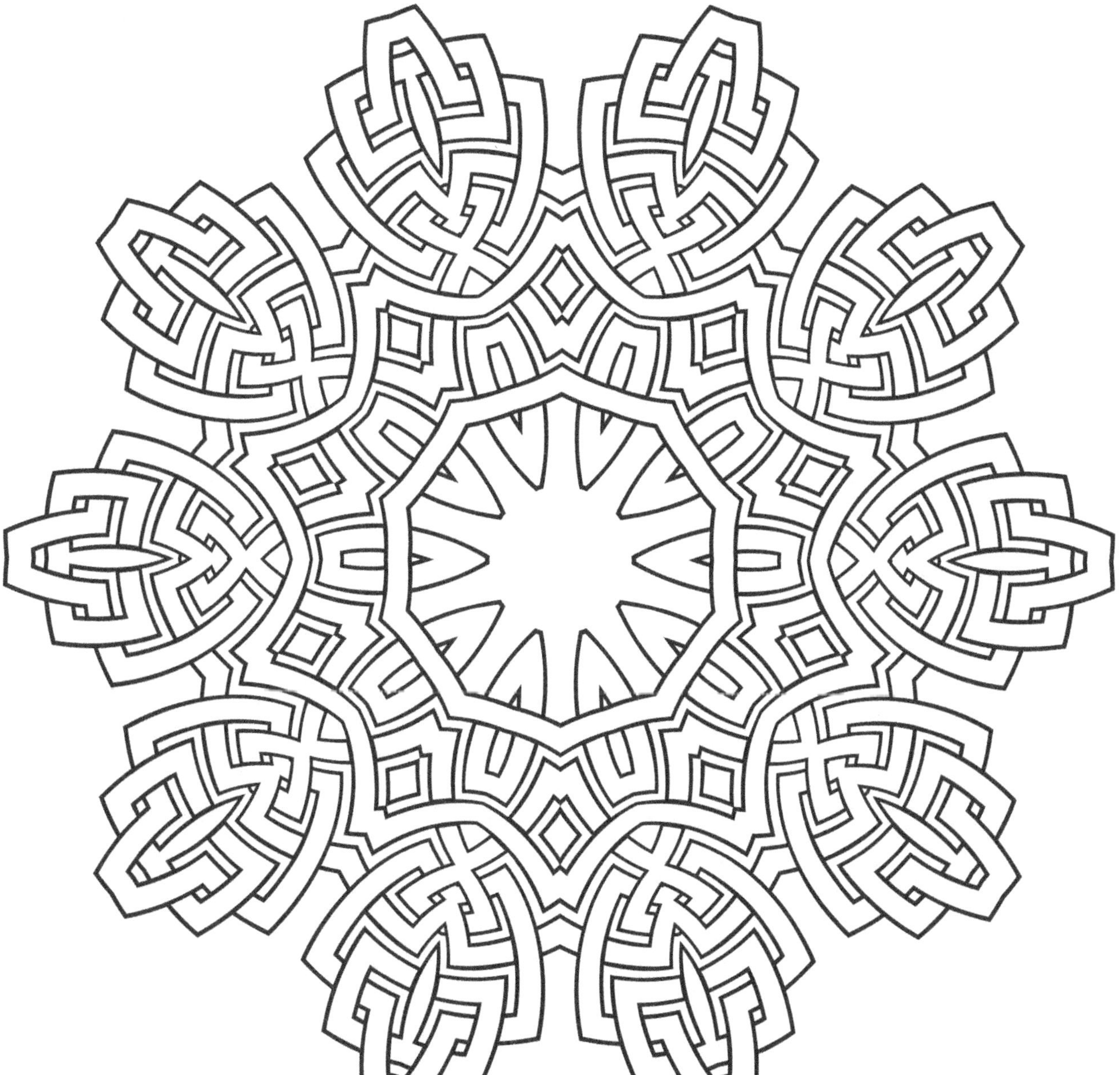

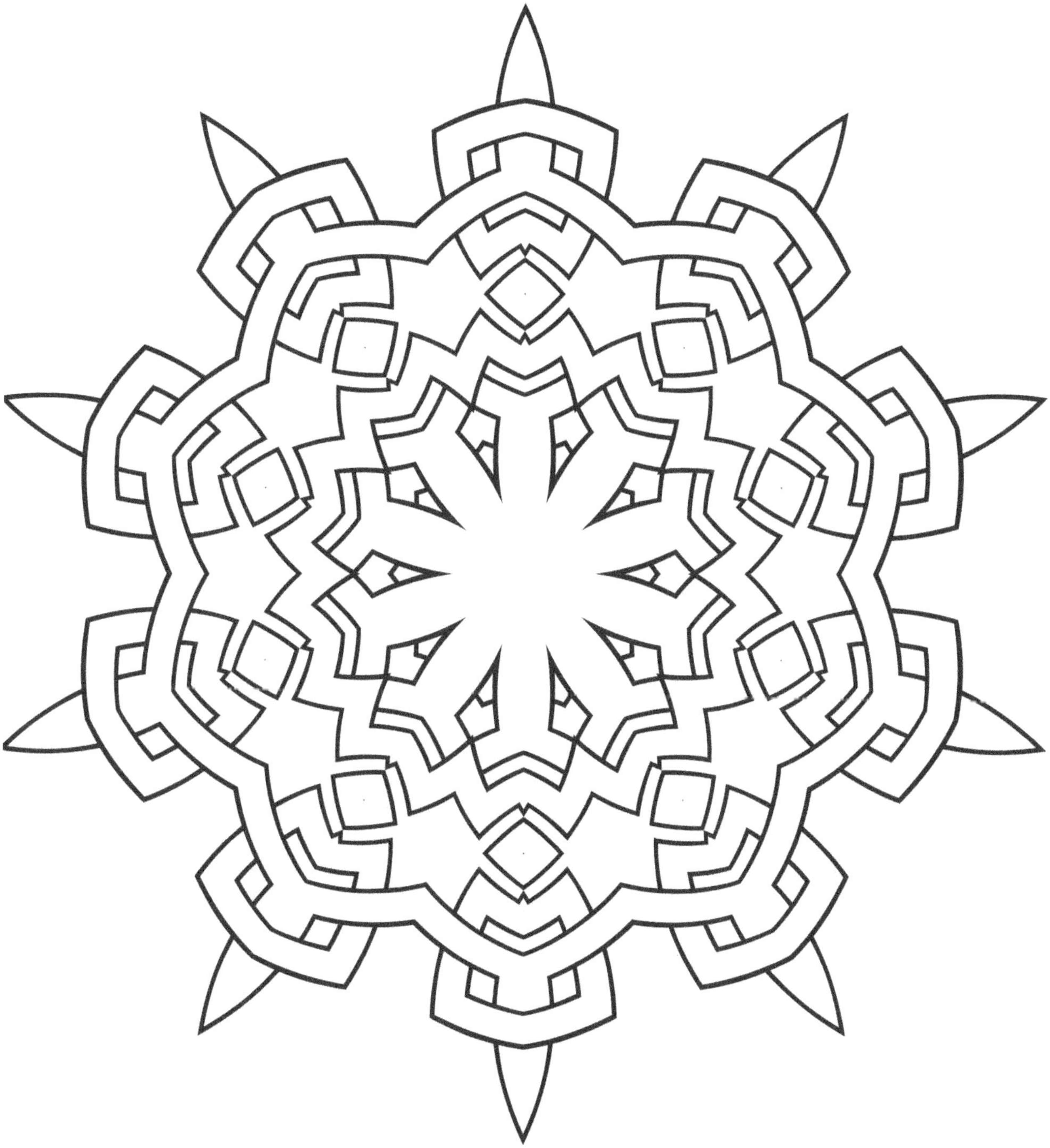

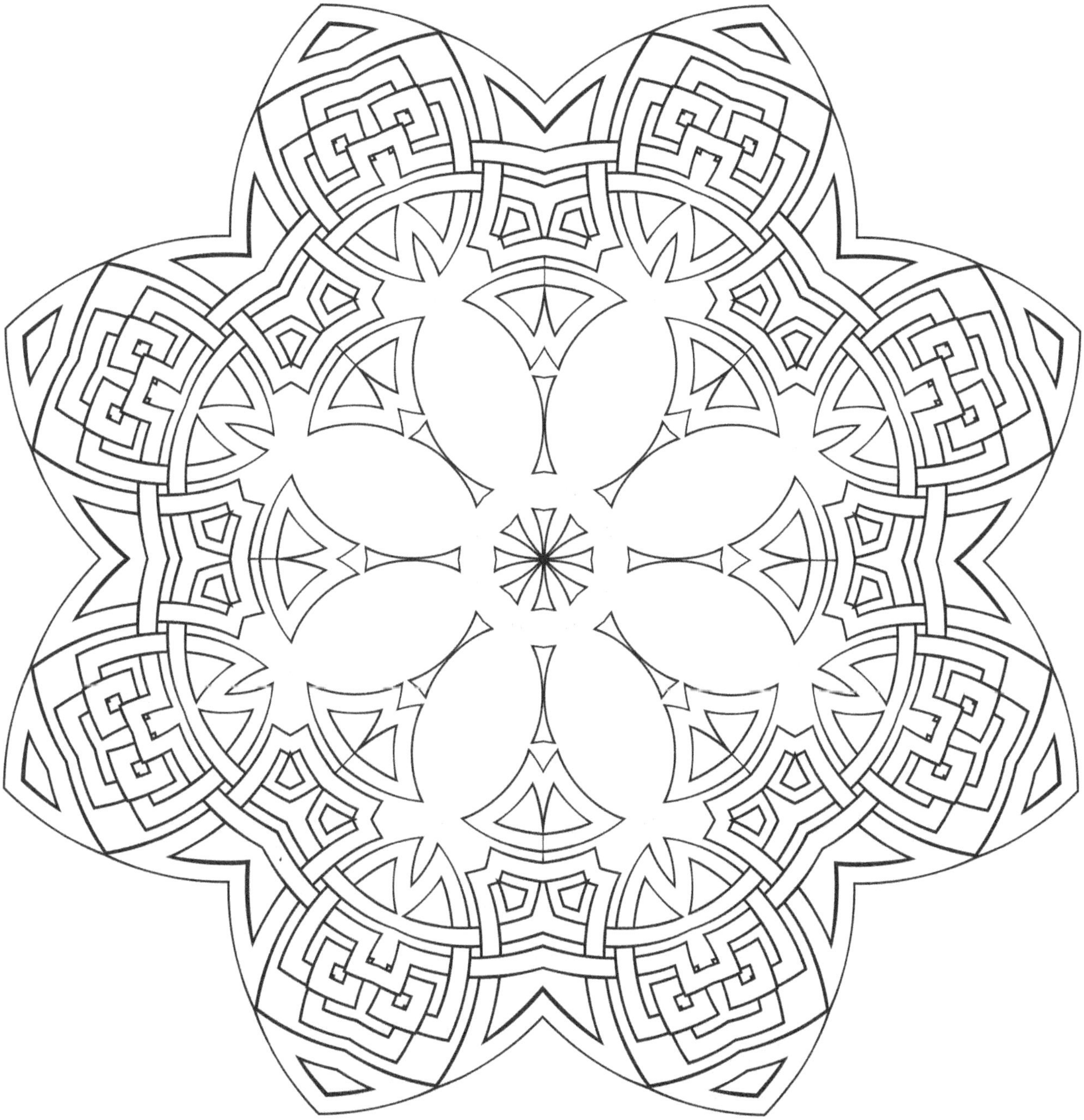

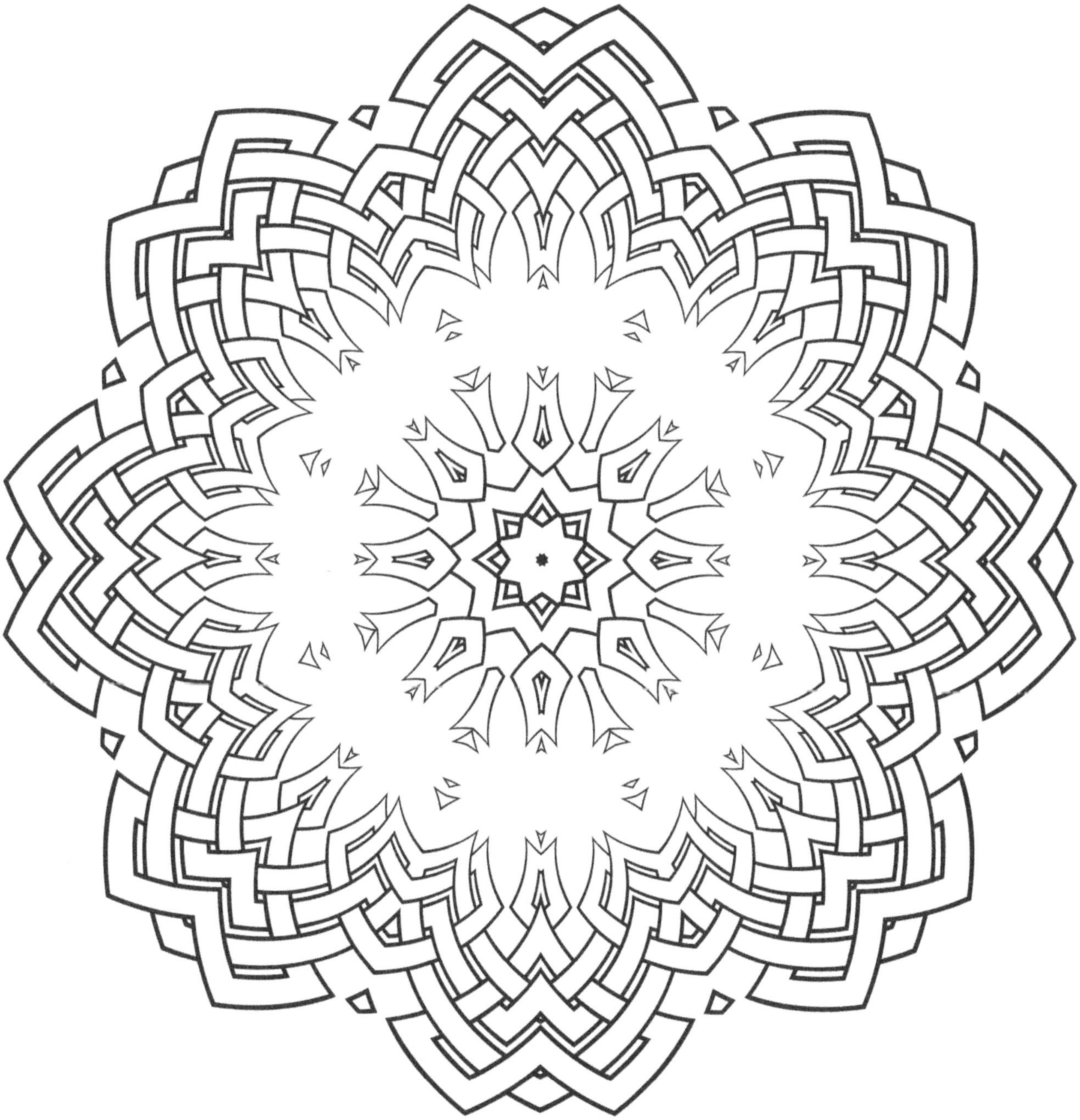

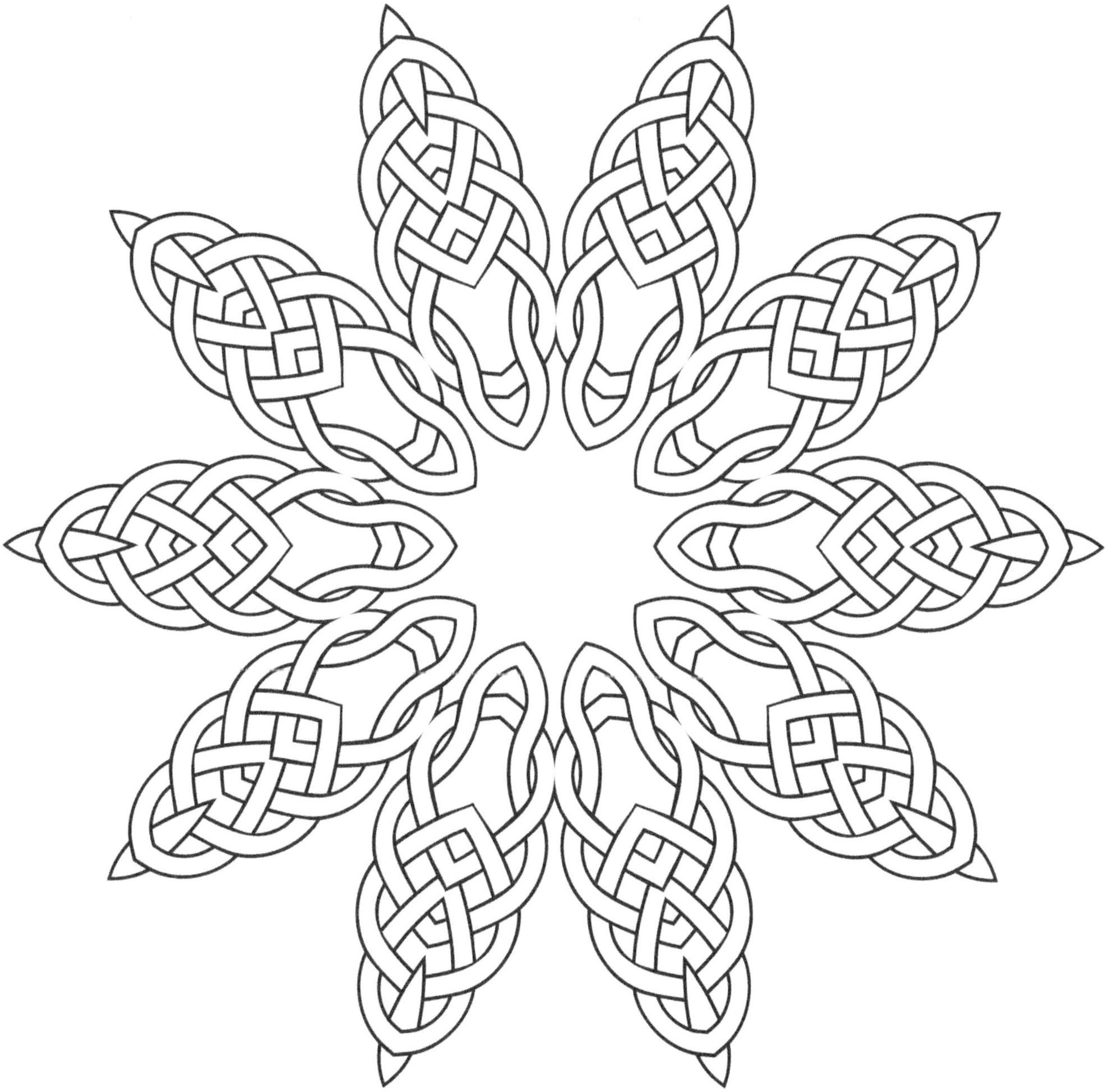

www.ingramcontent.com/pod-product-compliance
Lightning Source LLC
Chambersburg PA
CBHW080720190526
45169CB00006B/2454
* 9 7 8 1 5 2 3 6 5 2 5 0 1 *